ESSENTIALS OF
TOTAL
QUALITY
MANAGEMENT

The WorkSmart Series

The Basics of Business Writing
Commonsense Time Management
Effective Employee Orientation
Essentials of Total Quality Management
Goal Setting
Great Customer Service on the Telephone
How to Become a Skillful Interviewer
How to Speak and Listen Effectively
The Power of Self-Esteem
Productive Performance Appraisals
Resolving Conflicts on the Job
Successful Team Building

ESSENTIALS OF TOTAL QUALITY MANAGEMENT

Richard L. Williams

amacom

AMERICAN MANAGEMENT ASSOCIATION
THE WORKSMART SERIES

New York • Atlanta • Boston • Chicago • Kansas City • San Francisco • Washington, D.C.
Brussels • Mexico City • Tokyo • Toronto

This publication is designed to provide accurate and authoritative
information in regard to the subject matter covered. It is sold with the
understanding that the publisher is not engaged in rendering legal,
accounting, or other professional service. If legal advice or other expert
assistance is required, the services of a competent professional person
should be sought.

Library of Congress Cataloging-in-Publication Data

Williams, Richard L. (Richard Leonard), 1943–
    Essentials of total quality management / Richard L. Williams.
        p.   cm.—(The WorkSmart series)
    Includes bibliographical references and index.
    ISBN 0-8144-7833-6
    1. Total quality management.   I. Title.   II. Series.
HD62.15.W543   1994
    658.5'62—dc20
                                                    94-4851
                                                    CIP

Printing Number

10   9   8   7   6   5   4   3   2   1

To
Rhonda
my best friend and eternal companion

CONTENTS

ix **PREFACE**

1 **CHAPTER 1**
What Is TQM?

6 **CHAPTER 2**
Where Did TQM Begin?

16 **CHAPTER 3**
What TQM Isn't

23 **CHAPTER 4**
The Nature and Origins of Quality

34 **CHAPTER 5**
Quality Manufacturing or Quality Service?

43 **CHAPTER 6**
Implementing TQM in an Organization

56 **CHAPTER 7**
Six TQM Techniques

70 **CHAPTER 8**
TQM Tools

83 **CHAPTER 9**
Making TQM Work

95 **CHAPTER 10**
TQM Awards, Standards, and Certifications

101 **GLOSSARY OF TERMS**

105 **INDEX**

PREFACE

The ultimate purpose of Total Quality Management (TQM) in any organization is to improve the quality of that organization's products and services for the customer. This book has a dual purpose. The first is to help readers understand the basic philosophy and principles of TQM so they can make an informed decision whether to pursue this management approach in their organization. The second is to help supervisors, managers, and leaders understand the nature of TQM and be able to apply its principles to their departments and organizations.

TQM cannot be thought of as a quick fix that can be "installed" in the organization overnight. TQM is not a passing fad that can be learned quickly. It cannot be purchased from a vendor or consultant, or selected out of a training catalog. And it cannot be a half-hearted venture pursued by only part of an organization. TQM success demands total commitment from the entire organization.

It is imperative that more U.S. organizations adopt TQM as their corporate philosophy. Without a significant increase in both the manufacturing and service quality of American business to a world-class level, the companies in other countries that do embrace TQM could erode even more of the U.S. economy. As difficult as TQM might at times appear, it is far less difficult and far more desirable than national economic failure. TQM by itself cannot save the U.S. economy, but it can have a significant impact on the success of those companies that adopt its principles.

TQM is an American, not a Japanese, invention. The basic philosophy and principles were developed by Americans—Shewhart, Deming, Juran, and others—as I explain in the chapters that follow. Accepting TQM principles does not mean having to or endorse Japanese culture or methods. This book shows how TQM is a time-tested, realistic, and viable process that can be used to improve quality, and ultimately drive success through your organization as well.

Organizations with a TQM culture are not only more productive and effective but also are far more enjoyable places to work. This is because TQM makes both individual and organizational success more likely, while meeting human needs in the workplace. Indeed, TQM has great positive value for an organization, its customers, and its employees.

ESSENTIALS OF
TOTAL
QUALITY
MANAGEMENT

CHAPTER 1

WHAT IS TQM?

It's difficult to read a business publication today without coming across the words *TQM, quality,* or *Total Quality Management.* Yet in spite of the focus on these terms, not many people understand what TQM is—and, more important, what it will do and how it can be implemented.

It's the nature of American management to use buzzwords. These popular terms generate interest, focus attention, and signal change; and that's good. Without change any business soon stagnates and dies. So if buzzwords can make things better, why not use them?

America's incredible economic growth during the 1960s and 1970s created massive production and organizational structures. In too many industries, however, there also developed an emphasis on the *quantity* of goods produced rather than on the *quality* of products and services. Improved quality in similar goods from other countries, most notably Japan, soon led to a huge trade imbalance. To compete with these imports American industries returned to a much-needed concern for quality. Total Quality Management—or TQM for short—was introduced, and today its name reigns as the most common buzzword in the American workplace.

IS TQM A PASSING FAD?

Management is not an exact science. It is a field of endeavors that changes with the times, and its proponents seek out the interest and excitement of new concepts and techniques.

Because management is a constantly changing art, most managers are always looking for new techniques to make their skills more effective in solving today's problems.

As a result, American management tends to follow trends. *Team building, excellence,* and *empowerment* were key words of yesterday's business books, magazine articles, and seminars. Now *quality* and *TQM* are management's buzzwords.

Just as the principles of team building have lasted beyond its time as a buzzword, the principles that drive quality will also endure the test of time. TQM will prevail and become the standard by which organizations are judged.

IS TQM A PROCESS, A TECHNIQUE, A MANAGEMENT STYLE, A GOAL, OR A TOOL?

The answer to that question is Yes! TQM is all of those things—and more. However, TQM is mostly a style of leadership that creates an organizational culture which helps achieve the goal of creating the highest possible quality products and services.

The problem is that most managers see TQM as a simple tool or formula to be learned in a one-day seminar and then quickly implemented in a department or company. TQM doesn't have to be difficult, but there's very little about it that is quick or easy. Total Quality Management is mostly a process of creating an environment in which management and workers strive to create constantly improving quality.

IS TQM A REALISTIC GOAL FOR THE AVERAGE COMPANY?

If TQM isn't a realistic goal for an "average" company, then thousands of such companies will soon be frustrated in their efforts to implement these changes. Making TQM work may be a complex task, but it certainly isn't impossible,

When TQM is properly implemented, principles will add value and quality to virtually any organization.

especially for an average company. On the contrary, one of the best places to institute TQM principles is in average companies. Quality consultants have observed some of the most outstanding results in run-of-the-mill, average companies.

That does not mean, however, that TQM won't work in below-average or above-average organizations. Experience shows that the principles that drive TQM can add value to practically any organization, regardless of existing quality output. When TQM is properly implemented, principles will add value and quality to virtually any organization.

DOES "TOTAL" QUALITY MEAN "PERFECT" QUALITY?

The masterminds of goal setting warn of setting unrealistic goals that can't be achieved. In his best-selling book, *The Game of Work,* Charles A. Coonradt says, "Goals must be realistic and obtainable."[1] The goal of producing "perfect" quality might be unrealistic, and therefore an unobtainable goal. In the manufacturing and service industry, consistent perfect quality is difficult, if not impossible, to obtain.

Thus, TQM does not mean that an organization must seek perfection in all its products and services. Rather, it means achieving the highest quality of service and products possible, under the circumstances for that organization. TQM philosophy says that quality is not a fixed goal that is achieved, celebrated, and then forgotten; rather, quality is a moving target, and the goal is to constantly improve quality.

IS TQM WORTH THE EFFORT?

TQM has not been successfully implemented in every organization, just as excellence, team building, and empower-

1. Charles A. Coonradt, *The Game of Work* (Salt Lake City: Shadow Mountain Press, 1984), p. 23. (800) 438-6074.

ment have not been completely successful in every situation. Regrettably, some companies have given up TQM, others have scaled back their financial investment in and commitment to TQM.

But for every unsuccessful example, there are dozens of success stories. We don't hear enough about the success stories, unfortunately, and we hear too much about the failures. It seems to be the nature of some business publications to focus on failures. Rather, they should describe the successes. Managers need to respect the challenges of TQM, but not fear its failure.

Simply stated, the only limiting factor for implementation of TQM is the commitment of people in the organization. TQM works where people want it to work. Regrettably, it doesn't work where people don't demonstrate resolve and commitment to TQM. Remember, TQM is most definitely worth the effort!

WHAT IS THE DIFFERENCE BETWEEN AN "EMPHASIS ON QUALITY" AND TQM?

For TQM to work, it must become an integral part of organizational culture. TQM doesn't come from the efforts of a few committed individuals. It happens only when the vast majority—if not everyone—in an organization demonstrates a daily commitment to TQM principles. Casual talk from management about TQM is not TQM; the efforts of a minority are not TQM. TQM isn't an attachment to an organization; it's the foundation on which the organization rests.

The difference between an "emphasis on quality" and Total Quality Management is how much the TQM philosophy is woven into the fabric of the organization. A quality emphasis is often temporary; TQM is long term.

SO WHAT IS TQM?

The early development of TQM centered on three basic concepts: tools, training, and techniques. The tools were the counting systems that enabled manufacturing tolerances to improve; the training involved the level of quality awareness by everyone in the organization; and the techniques were the methods to improve the quality of products and services.

Over time we learned however, that focusing on tools, training, and techniques had only a limited impact on quality. Something was missing. Dr. Marshall Sashkin and Dr. Kenneth J. Kiser saw the broader implications:

> TQM means that the organization's culture is defined by and supports the constant attainment of customer satisfaction through an integrated system of tools, techniques, and training. This involves the continuous improvement of organizational processes, resulting in high quality products and services.[2]

TQM isn't a seminar or handbook on ways to change an organization overnight. It is management focused on customer satisfaction. As such, it must be implemented as a process throughout the organization.

2. Marshall Sashkin and Kenneth J. Kiser, *Putting Total Quality Management to Work* (San Francisco: Berrett-Kohler Publishers, 1993), p. 39.

CHAPTER 2

WHERE DID TQM BEGIN?

Total Quality Management had its beginnings with a Japanese invention called quality circles (QCs), sometimes referred to as quality control circles. The idea behind QCs was to bring workers together in regular weekly meetings to discuss ways of improving the workplace and the quality of work. Workers were encouraged to identify potential quality problems and then discuss and develop their own solutions. The first QCs started in Japan in 1962, and by 1980 there were over 100,000 QCs functioning in Japanese organizations.

QCs were imported to America in the 1970s and gained popularity in the 1980s. With their obvious success in Japan, QCs spread throughout American industry, with everyone's high expectations of immediate and dramatic results. They were so common that in 1986 *Business Week* described QCs as the fad of the 1980s.[1]

While QCs worked well in Japan, and had a positive impact on quality improvement in that country's industries, they met with only marginal success in America. In some situations, QCs even had a negative impact on quality. For the most part, their use died out in the United States by the late 1980s, disappearing almost as fast as they had appeared.

Why didn't quality circles work in America? Their failure was due more to the way they were used than anything inherent in the technique. American facilitators of QCs often treated the concept as a seminar—a feature that could be

1. "Business Fads: What's In–And Out," *Business Week,* January 20, 1986, p. 60.

"installed" in an organization. Speaking of such simple solutions to quality problems, W. Edwards Deming said, "A usual stumbling block [in improving quality] is management's supposition that quality control is something that you install, like . . . a new carpet."[2]

If used properly, quality circles not only improve quality but also increase employee involvement, innovation, and participation. The key, however, is the facilitator and the techniques he or she uses to build and maintain focus and direction for the group. The leader of a quality circle must be a skilled facilitator with exceptional interpersonal skills and abilities.

W. EDWARDS DEMING

Considered by most people to be the father of production quality and quality control, W. Edwards Deming was actually an industrial engineer. Deming recognized that workers were the only people in a position to actually control the production process. He developed what is known as the Deming Cycle: Plan, Do, Check, and Act (PDCA).

Although Deming was outspoken concerning methods of improving quality, in the early 1940s he was ignored by American industry leaders. Ichiro Ishikawa, head of the Japanese Federation of Economic Organizations, invited Deming to present a series of lectures to this influential organization of Japanese business leaders. Unlike American managers, these top Japanese managers accepted Deming's ideas. They realized that for Japan to prosper, its reputation for producing poor-quality goods would have to change. A new culture founded on quality production would have to be developed.

During the 1950s and 1960s, most Japanese companies quickly adopted Deming's principles of quality control. They established competitions and prizes for improved qual-

2. "Report to Management," *Quality Progress,* July 1972, p. 2.

ity. Workers became involved, and the quality of goods produced dramatically improved. Within twenty years, the reputation of Japanese products had changed, and Japanese manufacturing had come to stand for consistency in quality.

Deming's Fourteen Points

Half-hearted efforts at quality improvement do not produce long-lasting results.

In the course of his career, Deming began to focus less on tools, techniques, and training and more on what he called "a philosophy of management." He believed that TQM must be the foundation, the very roots, of a company. From this revolutionary thinking he developed his famous "fourteen points," and his "seven deadly diseases" that afflict American management. Briefly, the fourteen points are as follows:

1. *Create constancy of purpose for improvement of product and service.* The traditional American company has placed net profit or shareholder value as its primary priority. Deming stressed that quality must come first, and that profit is only a consequence of achieving quality.

2. *Adopt the new philosophy.* Deming said that adoption of a quality philosophy cannot be merely a function of the executive committee or the CEO. The philosophy must be a shared decision and responsibility assumed by everyone in the organization. Deming cautioned that half-hearted efforts at quality improvement do not produce long-lasting results.

3. *Eliminate dependence on mass inspection.* Quality cannot be an afterthought or something added to a company's processes. It must be the foundation on which the organization is based. Mass inspection of products assumes that quality can be achieved by identifying errors and correcting them, but this has proved to be untrue.

4. *Eliminate awarding business on price alone.* A profitable business obviously cannot ignore vendor pricing, but Deming insisted that acquisition costs should not be the primary or only concern. He said that supplier interests, concerns, and commitment to ultimate customer satisfaction should be

> **Whatever level of quality is realized today must be the basis for future improvement.**

the focus of attention. That, coupled with acquisition cost, form the basis of supplier selection.

5. *Institute constant improvement to the system of production and service.* Everyone in the organization must believe that what is good enough for today is not good enough for tomorrow. Constant improvement means that no standard or level of achievement can be binding on the future. Whatever level of quality is realized today must be the basis for future improvement. Established, unchanging standards are the death of an organization.

6. *Institute effective training.* Although Deming was originally concerned most with training in statistical quality control, he also taught that workers must be trained how to do their jobs. Worker training must be specific, related directly to the job, and equal to the responsibility. Deming emphasized the importance of production training for workers, rather than management development.

7. *Institute effective leadership.* Leadership for top management consists of developing and applying a strategic vision of a TQM culture. It involves constantly modeling the values that enhance such a culture. Leadership for line supervisors consists of using appropriate coaching techniques and providing timely training opportunities to assist workers.

8. *Eliminate fear.* Fear can be a critical stumbling block for implementation of TQM. When workers fear the effects of speaking out, taking risks, or asking questions, the possibility of improving quality is drastically reduced. Managers who rule by fear, through the administration of punishments or by granting special favors, create a climate of perceived unfairness. A concern for quality demands that workers feel reasonably secure in the organization.

9. *Eliminate barriers between departments.* Roger Tunks, president of the Richard-Rogers Group, has said that "Initially, competition between intact work groups can be exciting, but in the long run it destroys cohesion, morale and a desire to perfect the process." Traditional organizational structures can encourage competition between departments

and work groups. To achieve TQM, all workers must feel an overriding sense that quality is the goal, not competition with co-workers.

10. *Eliminate slogans and exhortations.* Deming was critical of people who believe that quality is a product of motivation or inspiration. He added that the motivational tactic can erode quality because it focuses attention on the "desire to," rather than the "how to." Deming once said that clever slogans put workers in the position of having a general idea where they ought to go, but no road map of how to get there.

11. *Eliminate numerical quotas.* An emphasis on production numbers or quotas encourages people to focus on "how many" rather than "how good" or "how effective." Too often, the goal becomes one of finding an innovative way to increase quantity instead of improving quality. Exceeding customer expectations regarding quality has far more long-term value than exceeding customer expectations with the quantity of product manufactured.

12. *Eliminate barriers to pride of workmanship.* Deming assumed that most people want to do a good job. They don't want to receive unjust criticism or be inaccurately judged. Their minimum expectation is to be treated fairly. Annual performance appraisals that focus on negative generalizations can destroy any desire for improvement. Thus, a TQM environment requires a management system that encourages workers to do their jobs well, and to the best of their ability, in contrast to a management system that attempts to get compliance through fear or intimidation.

13. *Institute a vigorous program of education and improvement.* Deming believed that workers must have a strong foundation in the tools and techniques of quality control. He said that tools and techniques are the language of quality; they are how we communicate and how we improve. But he added that it is crucial for workers to develop new methods of teamwork and of sharing, and to find new ways to achieve the new management philosophy, which is the TQM culture.

14. *Take action to accomplish the transformation.* A minority of workers cannot successfully implement TQM; even a simple majority of workers will likely fail at implementation. It takes commitment from everyone in the organization to successfully implement TQM. Top management must be concerned with the overall TQM strategy, and then take positive steps to make the strategy work. Workers alone cannot be expected to make TQM work.

Deming's fourteen points constitute his basic principles or philosophy of management, which he sometimes called his "operational theory of management." Although he developed the fourteen points over several decades, they are still considered the cornerstone of quality theory.

Deming's Seven Deadly Diseases

W. Edwards Deming was a realist. He knew that in bringing his quality philosophy to America he would be met with significant cultural and organizational opposition. He maintained that U.S. organizations were afflicted with seven deadly diseases, any one of which could spell doom to quality improvement.

1. Failure to provide adequate human and financial resources to support the purpose of quality improvement
2. Emphasis on short-term profits and shareholder value
3. Annual performance evaluations based on observations or judgments
4. The lack of management continuity owing to job hopping
5. Management's use of easily available data, without regard to what is needed to improve the process
6. Excessive health-care costs
7. Excessive legal costs

Some of Deming's diseases are obvious negative statements of his fourteen points. The first five diseases could be thought of as "basic management truths" because they are so much a part of most organizational systems. Nonetheless, Deming believed that for TQM to succeed, these seven diseases of an organization must be eradicated.

DR. JURAN'S APPROACH TO QUALITY

A focus on quality for the customer must be designed into every process and system in a company.

Joseph M. Juran, a contemporary of W. Edwards Deming, also had significant influence on the quality-improvement movement. His greatest contribution was his formulation of methods for creating a customer-oriented organization. Juran taught that a focus on quality for the customer must be designed into every process and system in a company.

Similar to Deming, Juran's approach involves a number of tools. Also, like Deming, he recognized that tools alone cannot automatically produce TQM. The power of the human mind to identify and correct problems is more effective than all the quality tools invested.

IS AMERICAN QUALITY ALL THAT BAD?

The key element here is time: Does the question refer to the manufacturing quality of today, or that of the 1970s and 1980s? Critics readily agree that U.S. manufacturing quality has been inferior to that of some other nations, most notably Japan. However, we cannot ignore the incredible strides that have been made in the past decade.

Most people who owned an American-made automobile of the 1970s and 1980s learned first-hand the problems that result when the manufacturing emphasis is on quantity, not quality. Owners of American-made automobiles in the 1990s have a different perspective, however. The big name-plates have turned to the theories of Deming and Juran, and have dramatically revamped their manufacturing processes. As the slogan for one company says, "Quality is Job One."

Many people feel that the quality of American cars produced today equals that of imports, and recent sales trends seem to support that notion. Of course, the quality revolution in America is certainly not complete. But other industries have begun their revolution, too, and others will certainly follow.

WHAT YOU CAN DO

Following are five statements about the origins of TQM. Rate each statement as it applies to your organization:

5 = Completely True   2 = A Little True
4 = Mostly True   1 = Not True
3 = Somewhat True

Rating

1. Management communications to workers deal mostly with methods of improving quality, rather than ways of decreasing expenses and improving profits.   _____

2. There is a shared commitment among workers, not just management, to improve quality.   _____

3. Our selection of suppliers and vendors is not based solely on low price.   _____

4. We strive for constant improvement with the quality of our products and services.   _____

5. The managers in our organization lead by example, and do not "rule" through fear.   _____

Total   _____

To score, add the points from the five statements:

20–25: TQM principles are working reasonably well.
15–19: TQM principles could be improved
Less than 14: TQM principles need improvement.

HINTS TO HELP, IF YOU SCORED LESS THAN 20 POINTS:

• Conduct an informal assessment of the written and verbal messages flowing from management to the workers. If the majority of information concerns short-term issues, such as cutting expenses or increasing profits, counter those messages with information about what quality is, why it is important, and how it can be achieved.

• Invest at least fifteen minutes each day working side-by-side with hourly workers to demonstrate your empathy for their efforts and to get closer to the issues. During these "side-by-sides," be sure to spend half the time listening to the workers' concerns and the remaining time sharing your beliefs about the importance of continuous quality improvement.

• Find out what criteria are used for the selection of materials and services from vendors. Can you modify or influence the priority of the criteria to emphasize the importance of quality? If not, can you ask probing questions to those who have the authority to modify the criteria?

• Continuous improvement is a philosophy that must permeate the very fabric of an organization. It isn't something you can fix overnight, but you can begin the process by doing everything possible to influence product and service standards to reflect the need for always improving standards. You can always expect more, something better, something stronger, and/or something that better meets customers' needs.

• Change in any organization must begin with one person and then spread to others as they see the benefits of the change. If there has been an inappropriate use of power and authority in your organization, you must set the course for a new direction involving leadership by example, management by principles, and discipline with respect.

CHAPTER 3

WHAT TQM ISN'T

Sometimes knowing what something is not helps one to gain a better understanding of what it really is. There has been enough discussion regarding TQM in the business environment that a brief explanation of some of the more common misconceptions might be helpful. This discussion isn't intended to be negative; it should help clarify the issues and show how TQM can be applied effectively.

BANNERS, POSTERS, AND SIGNS

In 1990, a plastics manufactuing company in the western United States began experiencing a dramatic increase in customer complaints regarding the consistency of its product. Over the course of thirteen months, the number of customer complaints regarding quality increased from an average of only three per day to over thirty-five per day.

The company had grown from a half-dozen employees working in a rented garage in the late 1970s to over 350 employees by 1990. The company's CEO said that the rapid growth had been a direct result of its ability to consistently deliver a higher quality product than the competition. While the majority of competitors struggled with product consistency, this upstart company, with only a handful of employees, captured a significant worldwide market share, and thus experienced remarkable growth in sales, employees, and profits.

In 1989 and 1990, however, quality problems escalated so quickly that additional people had to be added to the customer service department just to handle the increase in customer complaints, most of which focused on quality. To combat this sudden rise in quality problems, the CEO doubled the number of training hours for each person in the production line; but even this only marginally reduced the number of customer complaints.

In a staff meeting, one of the executives who had been with the company since its beginning suggested that too many of the new employees didn't understand the vision of the company's founders. It was his opinion that employees who had been with the company for several years still produced a high-quality product, but new employees lacked the ability and commitment to maintain high quality standards. This long-time executive then suggested that a banner be hung in the production area to remind all employees of the importance of shipping a quality product. Within a week a large banner was hung above the production line that read, QUALITY IS OUR GOAL!

Reflecting later on the banner and its impact on the employees, the CEO confessed that other than a few comments the first day, he didn't notice any behavior changes among employees. He and the other executives had expected at least some improvement in quality, but there was only minimal improvement from a few employees. So one large banner by itself, designed by management, had virtually no impact on quality in this plastics manufacturing plant. Experience has taught other manufacturers that simple posters and signs have limited impact on quality, if any at all.

QUALITY CIRCLES

Quality circles (QCs), which were discussed in Chapter 2, also do not necessarily improve product quality or services. Carefully conceived and implemented, and then integrated into an overall strategic plan of quality, QCs have been successful, however. Even though in the past decade many companies have discontinued QCs, owing to marginal or even negative results, quality circles can be an effective tool for increasing employee participation in the problem-solving process. QCs remain an untapped resource as part of an effective TQM approach.

TEMPORARY QUALITY CAMPAIGNS

Quality is neither temporary nor an accident.

Quality is neither temporary, nor an accident. There is little that can be done on a temporary basis to improve quality. Some managers have tried implementing a temporary quality program or campaign, usually including employee meetings, seminars, posters, slogans, badges, and articles in employee newsletters.

Quality is the product of an organizational culture that drives constant improvement and concern for producing high-quality goods and services. If employees believe that management's program is temporary, they will treat it as such. Product quality may improve somewhat after the temporary program has been "installed," but it will not remain at that new higher level, and it certainly won't continue to improve over time. Temporary or quick-fix programs are, at best, temporary.

MANAGEMENT TALK

It's difficult to pick up a business journal and not find some mention of quality or Total Quality Management. With so much talk about TQM, managers have begun to "talk the talk," perhaps in an attempt to be part of the latest business fad. It's likely these managers have a sincere desire for improved quality. But regardless of the motive, management talk about quality only increases awareness of the issue; talk alone cannot improve quality.

As with temporary quality campaigns, management talk can produce a brief improvement in employee efforts, but the results are short-lived and occur in only selected areas of an

Total quality comes only from a commitment by the entire organization.

organization. Total quality comes only from a commitment by the entire organization, not from efforts by isolated departments or divisions. Management talk just isn't enough.

Managers need to do more than just talk about TQM or improved quality. They have to "walk the talk." Their day-to-day actions do much more to create a climate for quality than all the talk they muster. And when a manager's "walk" conflicts with his or her "talk," most employees will believe and follow the "walk." As the saying goes, "actions speak louder than words."

SEMINARS AND WORKSHOPS

Some companies have attempted to install TQM through quality workshops or seminars that they have either developed in-house or purchased from an outside training vendor. Although these seminars may contain critical information for establishing a climate of quality, they are a quick fix. While many seminars and workshops certainly contain valuable information and techniques about quality, no training experience by itself can create a climate of TQM.

TQM seminars and workshops can be excellent sources of information and increased motivation. They cannot, however, be the primary vehicle through which a TQM culture is developed and sustained.

QUALITY CONTROL PROGRAMS

During the industrial boom of the 1970s and 1980s, many managers believed that the key to maintaining quality was a tough quality inspection or control program. After all, if only products that met tough standards were shipped, the quality must be good. The mass inspection logic sounded good at the time, and it was used by many manufacturers to ensure quality. For example, companies established tight manufacturing specifications and rigid inspection processes. Systems were geared to prevent inferior products from being shipped.

Some inspection processes apply standards during manufacturing, but most kick in after manufacturing is completed. Typical quality control programs don't permit or encourage improvement in the manufacturing process itself; they assume that current production standards and quality will be the same in the future. This system creates a bottleneck at shipping time. It's not uncommon for quality control goals to be in conflict with the production department's desire to ship at the end of the month. And it's equally common for compromises in quality to be made at those times.

A quality control bottleneck can be reduced or eliminated when the quality of product manufacturing improves. In other words, the need for rigid QC inspection will decrease as manufacturing quality increases. The dilemma some organizations face is to decide which comes first: higher manufacturing quality or tighter inspection standards? Actually, the former is easier and has a longer lasting effect.

For a quality control program to work in a TQM climate, it must be part of an overall quality culture, driven by an organizational desire for constant improvement, not by meeting rigid standards of quality or quantity.

WHAT YOU CAN DO

Following are five statements about what TQM is not. Rate each statement as it applies to your organization:

5 = Completely True   2 = A Little True
4 = Mostly True   1 = Not True
3 = Somewhat True

Rating

1. Quality improvement is a permanent
   part of our organization; it's not just
   a temporary slogan or campaign.   _____
2. Workers can see by management's
   actions that they really believe in the
   importance of improving quality.   _____
3. All departments in our organization
   are actively involved with quality improvement.   _____
4. Seminars and meetings that discuss
   quality in our organization are part of
   a larger strategic plan to improve
   quality.   _____
5. Quality inspection programs in our
   organization are driven by the desire
   to achieve constant quality improvement.   _____

                                    Total _____

To score, add the points from the five statements:

> 20–25: TQM principles are working reason-
> ably well.
> 15–19: TQM principles could be improved.
> Less than 14: TQM principles need improve-
> ment.

HINTS TO HELP, IF YOU SCORED LESS THAN 20 POINTS:

• Take a walking tour of your plant or facility. How many posters, signs, and banners extol the virtues of quality? Ask at least a dozen workers what they think the signs mean. Don't remove the signs after you discover that few workers pay

(continues)

any attention to them. Instead, take what you've learned to management meetings and be willing to push the cause of quality's being a part of every aspect or dimension of the organization, not merely on signs, posters, and banners.

• Talking about quality can set the stage for improvement, but talk alone isn't enough. You've got to be seen taking corrective actions to improve quality by your subordinates and other managers. It's not a bad idea to deliberately be seen by others taking these actions, to lead by example.

• It's not uncommon for complex organizations to include isolated "empires" that have built over many years by power-hungry managers and executives. These islands in the organization can be a serious threat to a comprehensive quality movement. You can take the time to court the leaders of the empires to better understand the significance of continuous quality. You can be a teacher, a mentor, a facilitator, and a catalyst for change.

• There are numerous one-day public workshops held in most cities on a variety of topics. Many companies regularly send a contingent of managers to these workshops as their management development effort. You can be a quality leader by asking for a comprehensive training plan for each manager to ensure that the workshops' content agrees with and matches your organization's need for continuous quality improvement.

• Conduct an assessment of the criteria used to determine product or service standards in your organization. Ask inspectors or persons involved with inspection: Who established the standards? How long have they been in place? Are the standards realistic? How often are they upgraded or improved? Compile what you learn and make a presentation in a staff meeting.

CHAPTER 4

THE NATURE AND ORIGINS OF QUALITY

Quality is a product of, and must be driven by, the culture of an organization. Culture is the body of values and beliefs shared by all members of an organization. Values and beliefs are first expressed by leaders and managers, primarily through their attitudes and behaviors. Over time, most employees adopt the attitudes and emulate the behaviors of managers and leaders, especially when it comes to producing quality products.

VALUES DRIVE CULTURE

In an organizational culture where TQM works effectively, the employees and management have made a conscious decision to provide quality products and services to their customers. It is viewed as an important value. Successful organizations work hard to define and communicate these shared values and beliefs. For TQM to work in an organization, quality must be specifically identified and adopted as one of the primary corporate values.

Values are matters or issues that a person or organization regards as important. They are principles important enough to be defended; they are the glue that holds the organization together, and the bedrock on which the organization rests. Employees learn about organizational values more through the actions of managers and leaders than from a framed list hung on the lobby wall. They either sense the existence of

23

strong organizational values or they don't; there isn't much middle ground.

Sam Walton, founder of the Wal-Mart chain, helped establish friendliness toward customers as a corporate value. In addition to friendliness, the Nordstrom family established a no-hassle merchandise return policy as a basic value for its department stores. Setting a high standard that has lasted since the mid-1950s, the Walt Disney Company established an interesting list of corporate values:

- Quality
- Conservation
- Learning
- Value
- Fun
- Curiosity
- Customers are "guests"
- Teamwork
- Family entertainment
- Patriotism

The Disney values built the framework for the Disney mission statement: "We create happiness by providing the finest in entertainment for people of all ages, everywhere." Critical to the successful implementation of TQM is the realization that the need for quality must be expressed as a corporate value. This is because values drive attitudes, and attitudes drive behaviors.

VALUES DRIVE BEHAVIORS

A person's values can influence his or her attitudes as much as does past experience. Corporate values also play an important part in determining the attitudes of people at work. Although personal or corporate attitudes are not easily defined, they are manifested in day-to-day behavior. Positive attitudes enable people to work together effectively, while negative attitudes create barriers to effective communication. It's difficult for most people to work with someone who has a "bad attitude." Conversely, it's easier to work with someone who has a "good attitude."

Both people and organizations succeed because of individual and collective behaviors. Highly successful people have a clear understanding of their personal values; likewise, a successful organization has an organizational culture founded on well-thought-out values. Corporate values must reflect the organization's mission statement or statement of purpose. Employees tend to feel psychological ownership of corporate values when they have been involved in the selection of those values. Even employees not directly involved develop a sense of ownership after they observe co-workers and management consistently heeding those values.

Unproductive behavior reflects destructive or random thoughts and ineffective or unclear motivation. On the other hand, productive behavior reflects a clear understanding of goals, roles, and procedures. Productive behaviors come from people who know what the goals are, what their role is in the group, and what procedures can be used to accomplish the task they are assigned. One role of the manager is to effectively and clearly communicate the organization's goals, roles, and procedures.

Quality is the result of positive employee behaviors.

BEHAVIORS DRIVE QUALITY

Whether quality is reflected in a product or a service rendered to the customer, it is the result of something that is done—an action, a behavior—by one or more employees. In other words, quality is the result of positive employee behaviors.

Psychologists define *behavior* as an action that can be seen, heard, or counted. Behaviors—or their results—can be counted, scored, and even graphed. This realization may seem elementary, but the concept of quality can be abstract at times. Most managers assume they know what quality is and perhaps even how it can be achieved. But their idea of quality is often not linked to specific behaviors. Indeed, business in America has demonstrated that quality is an illusive concept.

Maximizing quality and minimizing problems or errors are basically two different steps. First, specific behaviors that produce positive results must be identified; then, a feedback process must help workers repeat those positive behaviors.

THREE ELEMENTS OF TQM

There are three important elements make up TQM: tools, techniques, and training. Tools are the devices that identify and improve quality; techniques are the ways to use the tools; and training is the instructional and communications process that improves the worker's ability to understand and use those tools and techniques.

TQM Tools

Uncontrolled variation is at the root of most quality problems.

Tools alone cannot lead an organization to a successful adoption of TQM. They are only one element of a TQM philosophy. TQM tools must be developed and used with two considerations in mind. First, they document the existence and extent of variability, which is at the heart of TQM. Employees must understand that uncontrolled variation is at the root of most quality problems. Second, tools analyze and control variability so that random or unexplained fluctuations in quality do not have to be tolerated. It is possible for workers to understand the work processes, and then move to a level of controlling and improving these processes.

The most common TQM tool is the *control chart* (see Figure 1). This is a graphic display of the measurements taken during a process. The horizontal axis often represents time, such as hours or days, or indicates a manufacturing batch. The vertical axis represents magnitude or degree, such as how much or how many.

Figure 1. Control chart.

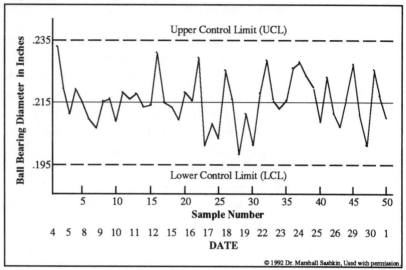

Control charts typically include three horizontal reference lines. The middle line, or baseline, is a standard reference from which variation is measured. The top horizontal line is called the upper control limit (UCL), and the bottom line is called the lower control limit (LCL). For example, the desired diameter of a ball bearing is .450, but an acceptable tolerance ranges from .400 to .475. The LCL would be .400 and the UCL would be .475. According to traditional thinking, any ball bearing manufactured within the UCL and LCL would meet an acceptable tolerance.

In a manufacturing situation, the measurement could be tolerances to a specification, such as thickness, size, or diameter, as with the ball bearing just mentioned. In a retail situation, a control chart could show the number of customers making a purchase each day. And in a sales situation, a control chart could demonstrate the number of sales presentations made each day.

Control charts only describe what has happened; they can't explain why it happened or what needs to be done to improve the process. The best tool for TQM is the human mind, which has the capacity to interpret why things happened and, most important, what must be done to make things improve.

Thus, the central issue of quality control is understanding and then controlling the amount of variability in the production process. The statistical tools merely document the variations; managers then identify methods to control and reduce product variability. But the proper use of TQM tools tends to generate improvement in itself. They often increase workers' self-confidence and their ability to repeat a correct process. The key to using tools effectively is enabling workers to see the results of their efforts. With adequate feedback, tools can be an important part of TQM philosophy.

Control charts are a visual representation of acceptable and unacceptable performance. When the data points are within the UCL and LCL, the variability is considered acceptable; and when a point is above or below the lines it is considered unacceptable. A well-designed control chart can be a daily reminder to workers regarding the quality of their work. Managers can use control charts to determine opportunities for coaching or praising worker performance. Control charts can also help eliminate the "putting out fires" response that consumes so much of some managers' time.

Effective implementation of TQM does not mean teaching all workers how to use tools. Rather, it is changing the way things are accomplished, through an entirely new system of leadership, management, and operation. Too often, an organization implements several traditional TQM tools, without the accompanying change in corporate culture. These attempts always end in failure because tools alone can produce only temporary quality improvements.

TQM Techniques

It's possible for managers to confuse TQM tools with the techniques to implement those tools. Techniques are the methods to improve quality, while tools are the specific devices used. For example, graphing the results of a process is a tool, but using the graphs in an employee brainstorming session is a technique. Statistical process control (SPC) is a tool, but getting employees involved in the decision-making process is a technique.

A tool is not effective without an equally effective technique. It's a waste of time and materials. Managers and supervisors must be aware of the differences between tools and techniques, to ensure the most effective implementation.

The Japanese have been successful in using a technique called participatory management, whereby employees are empowered to make decisions regarding how things are accomplished in their part of the organization. The logic of participatory management is that hourly employees are the closest to the problems—and to their possible solution. Involving employees in the decision-making process is a way of sharing responsibility to achieve success.

W. Edwards Deming made the Plan, Do, Check, Act (PDCA) cycle popular, although he attributed it to his friend and mentor, Walter Shewhart. This technique places the responsibility for action on the employee, after planning, doing, and then checking the results. The key ingredient in the PDCA cycle is delegation of responsibility and equal authority to act. Autocratic, top-down management systems are contrary to the PDCA cycle.

Employees brought together for a brainstorming session can be highly valuable in identifying solutions and improving communications. These groups are particularly productive when mixed, reflecting a variety of experiences, skills, and job positions. But brainstorming sessions require a talented facilitator to keep the discussion focused on the issues. And the size of the group is critical, with the effective units consisting of five, seven, nine, or eleven members.

Quality circles were discussed in Chapter 2. They can also be an effective technique for implementing TQM, but need to be carefully controlled, and participants must be thoughtfully chosen.

TQM Training

All TQM training must begin with an honest assessment of worker needs.

All TQM training must begin with an honest assessment of worker needs. Contrary to what happens in many organizations, the needs of trainers are not important. By matching worker needs with the right training methods and tools, the company gets workers who will be able to solve problems and improve work processes. It's important for the skills to be presented in the context in which workers will use them. Theoretical or abstract training only confuses the matter and obscures real issues. The real needs of the trainees must be the prime concern of the training effort.

Employee training in many American companies focuses on teaching people *how* to do something or *how* to operate equipment. In contrast, Japanese workers are encouraged to develop a relationship with the machinery they operate. It's common for employees to place personal signs on their machinery that illustrate their respect and even love for the machine.

The Japanese theory is that the highest quality work can be produced only when the human and mechanical elements work together with a common purpose. Japanese workers are first taught extensive cleaning procedures. Then they learn routine maintenance procedures, such as oiling, alignment, and calibration. The workers are taught how to perform preventive maintenance and soon become qualified to make more technical repairs. They become totally responsible for the inspection, operation, and repair of their machinery.

In contrast, some workers in Western cultures have so little respect for machinery they create a malfunction to reduce their work. Sabotage is a symptom of reduced respect not only for the equipment, but also for the organization and its workers and customers. The Japanese idea of a relationship between workers and equipment creates a bond of respect that significantly reduces equipment breakdowns.

SUMMARY

After World War II, W. Edwards Deming discovered that, despite extensive training of workers and engineers in the United States to use his tools and methods, there were only minor improvements in quality. Deming said of these unproductive postwar efforts, "I was lighting a lot of fires, but they were all going out."[1] The fires were going out because tools, training, and techniques alone do not drive TQM. It takes a commitment from the entire organization to neither stand still nor stagnate in mediocrity. Continuous improvement must be the theme for the entire organization.

WHAT YOU CAN DO

Following are five statements about the nature and origins of TQM. Rate each statement as it applies to your organization:

5 = Completely True   2 = A Little True
4 = Mostly True   1 = Not True
3 = Somewhat True

Rating

1. Workers are aware that quality is one of our stated corporate values.   _____
2. Workers in our organization had some influence in the formation of a mission statement.   _____
3. The workers in our organization are aware of how their daily performance impacts the quality of products and services.   _____
4. Our organization uses a combination of TQM tools and techniques in its strategic plan of improving quality.   _____

(continues)

---

1. David Halberstam, *The Reckoning* (New York: Morrow, 1986), p. 315.

Rating

5. Employee training in our organization centers on helping employees solve problems and improve their work processes. _____

Total _____

To score, add the points from the five statements:

20–25: TQM principles are working reasonably well.
15–19: TQM principles could be improved.
Less than 14: TQM principles need improvement.

HINTS TO HELP, IF YOU SCORED LESS THAN 20 POINTS:

• Within your area of responsibility, help workers identify a list of corporate values. Begin by asking what your organization stands for. Be sure to separate values from principles. Values are core issues like honesty and integrity. Principles are how values are integrated in daily activities, such as a policy that requires that customers that receive a refund within two working days.

• Within your area of responsibility, help workers formulate a mission statement. Get as many workers as possible involved. A one- or two-year *ordeal* is more effective and long-lasting than an overnight event. Workers will only feel ownership in the final product by believing they had some influence in the development of the statement. Begin by reviewing the organizational values, and incorporate them in the body of the statement.

• Help workers develop a feedback process that graphically demonstrates how their daily performance has a direct impact on the quality of products and services. Each employee, or group of employees if necessary, should have a line graph that helps them know if they are better today than they were yesterday. If you need help, read *The Game of Work* by Charles A. Coonradt.

• TQM tools and techniques work best when they are integrated in a strategic plan to drive continuous quality improvement. If your organization doesn't have a plan, either develop one for your area of responsibility or encourage your co-managers to jointly develop one with you.

• Conduct an audit of the employee training in your organization to ensure that it is based on specific behavioral objectives. Determine if the training includes definite methods for employees to identify and solve problems. Find out if the training does more than merely teach "how" things ought to be accomplished. Ensure that individual training elements are part of a comprehensive plan.

CHAPTER 5

QUALITY MANUFACTURING OR QUALITY SERVICE?

TQM is a total-organization process.

TQM got its start on the factory floor, and even today many managers define quality or TQM in terms of manufacturing consistency, manufacturing standards, or reduced variability. Certainly, there is a dimension of quality and TQM in those concepts, but there is another aspect that cannot be ignored: customer service. When an organization focuses on quality manufacturing and neglects how well products are delivered and customers are served, TQM principles are ignored. TQM requires continuity of quality that begins with the design or concept of the product or service and is carried through to servicing after delivery. TQM is a total-organization process.

REVOLUTION IN CUSTOMER SERVICE

Service, as a concern of American business, has undergone a dramatic revolution in the past decade. Although many organizations traditionally gave lip service to customer concerns, recently there has been more attention paid to delivering quality customer service. Unfortunately, this has occurred in only a few companies.

Experts in customer service predict that the service revolution will grow to include almost all industries. On the retail level, the focus is on providing customers with two types of stores: retail units that offer exemplary service and warehouse outlets with minimal or no service.

34

Business guru Tom Peters cites gasoline stations to illustrate this point. Before the 1970s, most stations in America offered full service. In addition to pumping gas, they often washed windows, checked oil and tire pressure, and even vacuumed the car. As late as the early 1980s, there were few self-service stations to compete with full-service stations. But as gasoline prices increased and consumers became more cost-conscious, the number of self-serve pumps grew, and today almost all stations are self-service. Most cities have only a few stations that will pump gas, let alone provide all the other services that were previously common.

Peters and other service experts believe that what happened to gasoline stations is occurring in other industries as price-sensitive shoppers polarize their shopping between price and service. Shoppers for most products will soon have to choose between low prices in a warehouse or higher prices in a total service environment. Companies will be forced to compete with either low prices or exemplary service.

CUSTOMER-DRIVEN QUALITY

In the mid-1980s, the CEO of a company with over 100 retail supermarkets and 25,000 employees was asked in a staff meeting why the company didn't conduct meetings with focus groups of customers to better understand their needs and expectations. Two other executives in the meeting quickly voiced their agreement that some type of customer input could be valuable. The CEO silenced the three executives, however, when he said, "There isn't a customer out there who can tell me anything about our business that I don't already know."

That company's profits continued to decline through the 1980s, until, after substantial losses, the parent company sold the division to a competitor. The CEO, all but one of the executives, and several hundred employees lost their jobs as a result. The CEO's comment in the staff meeting demonstrated his management style. His autocratic nature prevented conflicting opinions from being heard or nontraditional solutions from being tried.

The three executives must have felt that the company needed to get closer to its customers. Perhaps they saw that the quality of service could be improved through customer feedback. Perhaps they recognized that eroding profits could be related directly to the quality of service offered. Perhaps they had a solution that could have saved the company.

Customer-driven organizations develop processes to listen to customers. Listening to customers means more than conducting a customer survey every few years or reading the comments from a customer suggestion box. It means designing organizational processes that specifically reflect customers' needs, desires, and expectations. It means on occasion actually involving customers in the decision-making process to ensure that their views are incorporated into organizational procedures. When customers provide input to an organization, they quickly focus on selection and quality of products and services, the ease of doing business with the organization, prices and terms, and service warranties. Without customer input, organizations typically focus on ways to improve profit margins, decrease expenses, and protect the company from customers. The difference between these two philosophies is substantial and dramatic.

In contrast to the supermarket example where the CEO refused to listen to customers, there are other retailers that make a consistent effort not only to listen to customers, but also to implement changes they suggest. There are many examples of individual stores and entire chains that make every attempt to get close to customers.

But getting close to customers isn't enough. Highly successful retail stores have developed a habit of empowering customers to be virtually the boss. It's not uncommon for the manager in a successful store to conduct customer focus groups on a weekly or biweekly basis. In these sessions customers are encouraged to suggest changes about what products are stocked, how they are merchandised, pricing, and how employees can improve service. Other stores use customer suggestion boxes and comment cards to solicit customers' opinions.

The success of truly customer-oriented business is growing, which illustrates that the quality service revolution is taking place in America. There is no doubt that the demand for quality customer service will continue. Retail organizations that recognize this fact and make appropriate changes to improve quality will survive; those that don't, will not survive.

CUSTOMER SURVEYS AND ASSESSMENTS

There are many ways to listen to customers, but one of the most scientific is the customer survey and assessment. Customer surveys have been used for decades to improve service quality. Recent surveys, however, are in more depth and provide more detailed information.

The Customer Satisfaction Assessment Inventory (CSAI),[1] for example, defines specific employee behaviors that drive customer satisfaction and then asks employees to report on how frequently they observe other employees demonstrating those behaviors. The CSAI graphs the results on sixteen different dimensions so that management can see what specific positive behaviors are producing customer satisfaction and which negative behaviors are detracting from customer satisfaction.

Many companies survey customer attitudes and perceptions via either professional or in-house instruments. The value of the data received from customers is directly related to the design of the instrument. Although there is some value in all

1. Richard L. Williams and Dr. Marshall Sashkin, *Customer Satisfaction Assessment Inventory* (Salt Lake City: Vision Publishing, 1992).

surveys, the best data is obtained from an instrument that has been professionally developed. Surveys that focus on employee behaviors that meet or exceed customer needs and perceptions are most useful.

Customer focus groups appear to be easy to organize and conduct, yet many organizations don't use them. In actuality, assembling a dozen customers can be easy or difficult, depending on the location and willingness of customers. Selecting customers who will be honest and open in their assessment can also be difficult. Lastly, finding an experienced facilitator to conduct the session is a key to its success.

Focus groups can be useful ways of documenting current customer needs and expectations. As a side benefit, they communicate to customers that the organization is attempting to improve the quality of its service. Not only do retail companies benefit from customer groups, but wholesale and manufacturing organizations do as well. A large medical products manufacturer with only a hundred dealers as customers, for example, conducted three focus groups and discovered many easy and inexpensive ways it could improve service. Other companies have also received valuable results by asking customers how their service could be improved.

It's common to use suggestion boxes as a way of allowing employees to comment on company operations. Some companies also use suggestion boxes or comment cards to solicit customer comments. Although most comments are complaints, they can provide valuable information regarding customer feelings and perceptions.

Obviously, suggestion boxes are only valuable if they are used. A telecommunications company in the West lost the key to the employee suggestion box, and so the box wasn't opened for almost three years. A new manager worried that there might be three-year-old suggestions in the box, so she had a locksmith make a new key. Very quietly, and behind closed doors, the box was opened, only to find it empty. For almost three years not one of the seventy-five employees had made a suggestion. Contrast that to a steel mill that receives an average of fifteen suggestions a day from its 500 employees. In other words, each employee makes an average of almost eight suggestions a year.

The difference in these two examples lies in what people believe happens to their suggestions. Employees in the telecommunications company did not believe anything would change if they made a suggestion. Employees at the steel mill believed they could make a difference with their suggestions.

Great managers learn how to "work the floor." In many organizations the hourly employees are closest to the customers. In fast-food and many retail companies, part-time employees are the closest. Often managers are required to perform so many administrative duties they don't find time to see what's actually going on. Executives at Nordstrom's are required to work a certain number of hours each year as a salesperson. This is an excellent way to get corporate decision makers in a position to deal one-to-one with customers. TQM in a service organization must include a process where management regularly gets close to the customers. Thus, TQM in a service organization must include a way for management to get close to the customers.

Exceeding customer expectations for quality service must be an organization's driving force, its central concern, and its reason to be in business.

SUMMARY

Exceeding customer expectations for quality service must be an organization's driving force, its central concern, and its reason to be in business. This is true, not just for the manufacturing department or the customer service department, but for the entire organization the focus at every level and in every process must be on knowing and exceeding customer needs and expectations. Quality service isn't a goal, it isn't an objective; rather, it's a way of doing business, a way of life. Service is the purpose of business. And it's the only way to survive and prosper.

WHAT YOU CAN DO

Following are statements about manufacturing and service quality. Rate each statement as it applies to your organization:

5 = Completely True   2 = A Little True
4 = Mostly True   1 = Not True
3 = Somewhat True

Rating

1. Our organization pays as much attention to providing superior customer service as it does to monitoring product quality. _____
2. Many decisions in our organization are based on what has been directly learned from customers. _____
3. Our organization teaches employees in direct customer contact how to more effectively listen to customers. _____
4. Our organization frequently meets with focus groups to learn more about customer needs. _____
5. Our organization distributes surveys or assessments to customers in order to learn more about customer needs. _____

Total _____

To score, add the points from the five statements:

20–25: TQM principles are working reasonably well.
15–19: TQM principles could be improved.
Less than 14: TQM principles need improvement.

HINTS TO HELP, IF YOU SCORED LESS THAN 20 POINTS:

• Contact fifteen recent customers, either in person or on the phone, and ask: "If you could change anything about your recent transaction with us, what would it be? What one thing should we have done to better meet your needs? On a scale of one to ten, with ten the highest, how "delighted" are you with our product or service? If you owned this company, what's the first thing you would change?" Tabulate the responses and make a presentation in a staff meeting.

• Prepare a list of recent decisions that have been made in your organization. Invite several customers to attend a focus group meeting. Ask the customers to candidly comment on the decisions, whether they appear to affect the customers or not. Tabulate the responses and make a presentation in a staff meeting.

• Ask fifteen direct-customer-contact employees what the organization has done in the past twelve months to help them better listen to customers. Remember, listening is a learned skill, and many people are less than effective listeners. If you learn that some of the employees have not recently been helped with their listening skills, challenge the person responsible for skills training to develop such a program.

• Conduct a survey to determine how many customer focus group sessions have been held in your organization in the past five years. If there haven't been many, ask your co-managers how the organization can become customer-driven if customers aren't given an opportunity to express their opinions.

(continues)

• Find out how many written surveys or customer interviews have been administered in the past five years. If there haven't been many, ask your co-managers how the organization can become customer driven if customers aren't given an opportunity to express their opinions.

CHAPTER 6

IMPLEMENTING TQM IN AN ORGANIZATION

W. Edwards Deming said that TQM cannot be "installed" in an organization the way "carpet is installed in a new house." If TQM cannot be installed, then successful implementation must be achieved in other ways. The heart of TQM is understanding what those ways are; the secret of TQM is knowing how to use them.

Implementing TQM has two basic requirements. First, there must be a good working knowledge of the organization—how things really happen, who makes things possible, and what has to occur for goals to be accomplished. Second, people must have a good foundation in TQM—what it is, what it isn't, and how it works.

RESISTANCE TO CHANGE

If workers are unwilling to accept change, any attempts at TQM will have little chance of working.

It is natural for people to resist change. We all function well in a comfort zone, and feel threatened when asked to do something outside our zone of comfort. When threatened, people often resist change, and many fight to prevent that change from happening to them or to their organization. Resistance to change can be a problem because successful implementation of TQM often requires significant changes in thinking and action. If workers are unwilling to accept change, any attempts at TQM will have little chance of working.

43

Workers are more willing to accept organizational change when they trust management.

Even though deep down most people realize that change is necessary to keep up with the competition and a changing society, they nonetheless fear the effects of change and frequently do anything to prevent it from altering the way they live. In other words, most people perceive change egocentrically—from their own point of view. And they are more concerned with how that change will affect them personally than with what the change could do for the organization.

Fear of change takes many forms, but the fear of a change in working conditions ranks high. The threat of possible unemployment also causes fear. As a result, any minor change in organizational procedures or working conditions can be a major crisis for some workers.

To demonstrate how people react to change, ask a few people the following question. "How would you feel if I told you that I'm about to announce a change that will affect you and the organization in the very near future?" The responses will fall into three general categories:

1. They will respond positively to the impending change, saying, "A change might be good."
2. They will want a clarification on how much the change will affect them and their position, asking, "What exactly do you have in mind?"
3. They will fear even any suggestion of change, saying "Every time something changes around here, I get the short end of the stick. I don't like change."

Workers are more willing to accept organizational change when they trust management. There are four ways a manager can develop trust and sell the importance of accepting a change. First, explain the specific benefits that come from the change, and the consequences of holding to the status quo. Second, explain frequently *why* things happen as they do, rather than telling only *how* things ought to be done. Third, tell the truth; deception is easily recognized by most people. Fourth, take time to relate to the workers; the more a manager knows about his or her employees, the more willing they will be to accept new ideas.

CONDITIONS FOR IMPLEMENTING TQM

Typically, large organizations are overstructured, with multiple layers of supervision and management. Established organizations are frequently overburdened with years of tradition and resistance to change. Thus, complex management and adherence to tradition can be deadly obstacles to successful implementation of TQM. It is not necessarily more difficult for TQM to work effectively in a large organization, but it certainly can be.

Successful implementation of TQM in a large, established organization must begin with an honest assessment of the situation. If the organizational climate is fundamentally contrary to the idea of empowering employees and delegating authority, then perhaps TQM isn't appropriate at this time. If, on the other hand, the organizational climate is reasonably consistent with TQM philosophy, or could be adapted to TQM philosophy, then the chances of successful implementation are greatly increased.

Small companies can be incredibly simple, with little or no formal structure, or they can be unbelievably complex. The difference has to do with the history and evolution of the organization as well as the personality of top management, particularly the founder or CEO. Entrepreneurships tend to take on the personality and characteristics of the entrepreneur. If those traits are conducive to a TQM environment, implementation could be successful. If, however, the entrepreneur's personality does not permit basic TQM elements such as empowerment and delegation of authority, any implementation could be a serious struggle.

The key to successful implementation of TQM in a small, new organization is the CEO. If the CEO demonstrates firm commitment to TQM, in both words and actions, success can almost be guaranteed.

IMPLEMENTING TQM IN ANY SIZE ORGANIZATION

The methods to implement TQM are as varied as organizations themselves and hinge on the abilities, knowledge, and experience of the persons involved. Because TQM is a complex process, techniques differ. There is no standard or perfect process, nor is there only one way to achieve TQM. Nonetheless, many consultants follow a five-step process that has been successful for many organizations. At this point, it represents the best thinking on making TQM the core of an organization's culture.

Step one: Culture assessment. Conduct an honest assessment of the organization's culture. This can be done by someone in the organization or a consultant with extensive TQM experience. The point is to make an objective assessment and accurately identify how the culture functions in the organization. Since a culture will either accept TQM principles or reject them, the key is to make that determination before proceeding with the next steps.

The inventory developed by industrial psychologists Marshall Sashkin and Kenneth Kiser can help assess an organization's ability to adapt to TQM principles.[1] The TQMAI has three primary dimensions: culture, tools and techniques, and concern for customer quality. When administered to sample workers, managers, and executives, the instrument assesses the degree to which the organization's existing culture supports TQM principles (see Figure 2).

The tools and techniques dimension measures the existence or potential integration of TQM tools and techniques. Respondents estimate the extent to which these tools and

1. Marshall Sashkin and Kenneth J. Kiser, *Total Quality Management Assessment Inventory (TQMAI)* (Seabrook, MD: Ducochon Press, 1993).

Figure 2. Results from the TQMAI are displayed on a triangular graph that illustrates the extent to which an organization will adapt to TQM principles. This organization's culture would easily adapt, but workers understand and use few TQM tools and techniques.

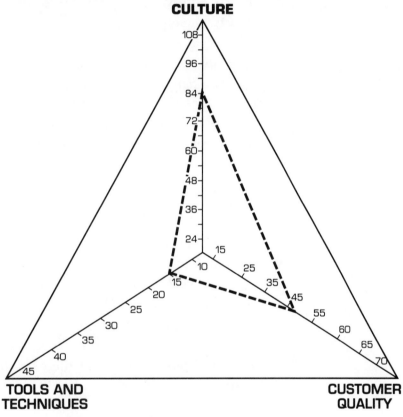

Source: © 1992 Dr. Marshall Sashkin. Used with permission.

techniques are used in the organization and the degree to which TQM-related training is available. The customer dimension assesses how well concern for quality is built in to the organization's operations. The cultural dimension measures eight elements important in supporting and sustaining a quality movement:

1. Measurement for improvement
2. Authority equal to responsibility

3. Rewards for results
4. Teamwork and cooperation
5. Secure jobs
6. Fairness
7. Pay equity
8. Ownership

Step two: Executive training. Conduct a training process for top leadership. This training is best scheduled in six to eight short sessions over a period of at least three to four months; participants can then more easily absorb the potential impact of TQM implementation. The training should consist of six elements:

1. A basic summary of what TQM is, what it will do, and what it will not do
2. The purpose and intent of TQM in a service or manufacturing organization
3. Why TQM is so important in today's marketplace
4. An overview of TQM principles
5. A description of the commitment required from the entire organization to make it work effectively
6. A written statement of the executive group's vision of what quality should be.

The executive-level training must be conducted by someone with not only knowledge and understanding of TQM but also facilitation skills to communicate the importance of the message. It is not uncommon for a few executives to resist conversion to TQM philosophy, or even to place additional emphasis on improved quality. The facilitator must be able to identify any hold-outs, and in concert with the CEO, deal effectively with the problem. The CEO must play an active role in these training sessions to demonstrate his or her commitment to the principles and the process.

Step three: Quality council. Establish a quality council composed of between twelve and twenty members. The members should be from all levels of the organization: top management, middle management, and hourly employees. As many departments, divisions, and regions as possible should be represented. This wide variety of experience and ability will help promote an operational synergy for the group.

The council's purpose is to first identify any potential barriers that could hamper adoption of TQM philosophy, and then to devise methods of eliminating those barriers. Most quality councils of this size can be a challenge to control, so a talented facilitator is necessary to ensure cohesive purpose and functional harmony. There are many consultants capable of providing this facilitation, or an experienced in-house person could be used.

It is possible that the council's methods could be contrary to the organization's established policies, procedures, or traditions. This means that the council must be empowered to institute change in the organization. Empowering a council of employees to make necessary changes to implement TQM is a significant switch from traditional management. Nonetheless, if changes are necessary, they must be made. Initially, a few people in the organization may feel threatened by the changes, but good communications can help reduce potential negative feelings.

The CEO could act as chairperson, or that responsibility could be delegated to another council member. The chairperson must have enough organizational power and authority to make difficult decisions, control the group, and resolve sensitive problems. It's not uncommon for one or more council members to become defensive regarding impending changes to operational procedures or department alignments. The chairperson must be capable of dealing with these issues fairly, without losing sight of the ultimate goal of TQM. In almost every organization there are long-established policies or procedures that must be modified or even

Empowering a council of employees to make necessary changes to implement TQM is a significant switch from traditional management.

eliminated to create a working climate for TQM. The chairperson, in concert with council members, must openly discuss possible solutions without regard to personal interests.

Three council members should be assigned to serve as a steering committee to monitor the council's progress and direction. Large groups occasionally become sidetracked on peripheral issues. If the council invests a substantial portion of its time in nonrelevant issues, its ability to tackle difficult problems could be hampered. Therefore, the steering committee should ensure that the TQM goal remains in the forefront of discussions and decisions.

Most quality councils typically use standard operating procedures, such as a recording secretary to document motions and discussions. Although a formal structure isn't necessary, many groups feel more comfortable with such clear guidelines.

Step four: Information dissemination. The quality council establishes a communications process to disseminate its information. One member of the council is assigned responsibility for ensuring that communications are effective and information reaches all levels of the organization. This person gives a brief verbal report on communications at each council meeting.

It's important that the quality council not function within an information vacuum; that alone can obstruct successful implementation of TQM. For this reason, it is vital that council members be willing to share information on their decisions. Obviously, there will be a few sensitive decisions that must be held in confidence for a period of time, but generally workers at all levels should believe they are receiving timely and accurate information. If the rumor mill provides more information about impending changes than does the council's communications, support for TQM might be weakened.

There are several methods of communications that can

be used by the council, and the best is to use a number of strategies. Memoranda and articles in company magazines are not sufficient. Research has shown that few employees regularly read company information. Depending on how the organization is geographically situated, it may be necessary to conduct small employee meetings to clarify what is happening in the quality council. Regardless of the medium used, the CEO and other key executives must be seen and heard endorsing the change to improved quality.

The communications process should be varied in method of delivery from time to time, to ensure that as many employees as possible understand what TQM is, and why it is so critical to the future of the organization. The increased communications should be frequent and continue throughout the TQM implementation. Consideration should be given to continue the increased communication well beyond when success is realized.

Step five: Integration. The final step is an integration of TQM tools, techniques, and training in the organization. TQM tools and techniques are discussed in greater detail in Chapters 7 and 8. There is no formula to define in what order or to what extent the three elements must be incorporated, because each implementation must be customized. Tools are used by management and workers, while techniques are primarily for management. While skill training is often intended for workers, it can be beneficial for management. The assessment process in step one will determine the existence of TQM tools and techniques in the organization. This knowledge can greatly help integration of additional tools and techniques.

Because TQM is a long-term process, the integration of tools, techniques, and training must also be planned in a large context. Organizations typically plan and budget development and skills training annually. Successful implementation of TQM requires a long-term commitment to the use of tools, techniques, and training.

CREATING A TQM CULTURE

Without strong cultural support, TQM becomes just another program, almost certain to fail. It is important, therefore, to understand what organizational culture is, how it is created, and how it can be modified.

A company's culture consists of basic organizational beliefs and values that are specifically defined and expressed by its leaders and managers, and then shared by the participants in that organization. In an article in *The Wall Street Journal,* John Urquhart has provided one of the best descriptions of organizational culture: "Culture is the cumulative perception of how the organization treats people and how people expect to treat one another. It is based on consistent and persistent management action, as seen over time by employees, vendors, and customers."[2]

A culture that drives and sustains quality is definitely not an overnight, off-the-shelf, one-size-fits-all creation. Culture must be carefully developed, nurtured, and sustained. Every organization has a culture, whether it has been carefully calculated or left alone to evolve by itself. Culture includes the folkways, mores, institutional ways, and taboos that define what is important to the organization and how things ought to be accomplished. A culture that includes a drive for improved quality will stress the highest possible order with every transaction and relationship.

Culture can be created or altered only by the leadership of the organization. The first step in TQM implementation is to gain whole-hearted support and commitment from the board of directors, CEO, and other company leaders. Without that uniform support and commitment, TQM will not succeed.

TQM leadership must be top-down, preferably from the CEO. If the CEO is not totally committed to TQM, there

2. John Urquhart, "Canada May Let Mail Workers Buy Shares in Agency," *The Wall Street Journal,* May 1, 1992.

must be a unified demonstration of support from the executive committee. It can only be hoped that the CEO will see the wisdom of TQM and become committed. Getting commitment from top-level leaders may also be difficult, but it certainly isn't impossible. A wide base of support is difficult for top executives to ignore. For example, middle managers have generated top-level interest in TQM by circulating articles and books on the subject.

WHAT YOU CAN DO

Following are statements about implementing TQM in an organization. Rate each statement as it applies to your organization.

5 = Completely True   2 = A Little True
4 = Mostly True   1 = Not True
3 = Somewhat True

Rating

1. Our organizational culture does not resist change in the way that things are accomplished. _____
2. Our organization does not have traditions that would get in the way of implementing TQM. _____
3. The culture of our organization is such that employees could be given increased authority and responsibility to improve quality. _____
4. By their actions, it is obvious that the leaders of our organization have a clear vision of what TQM is and how it can be implemented. _____
5. The communications process in our organization provides workers with prompt and accurate information. _____

Total _____

(continues)

To score, add the points from the five statements:

> 20–25: TQM principles are working reasonably well.
> 15–19: TQM principles could be improved.
> Less than 14: TQM principles need improvement.

HINTS TO HELP, IF YOU SCORED LESS THAN 20 POINTS:

• You can assess resistance to change in your organization by honestly considering the reaction from employees to the last half dozen staff or organizational changes. Additionally, ask a dozen employees what their first reaction is to changes in the organization. Be especially sensitive to responses that revolve around fear or "Oh no, here we go again."

• Make a list of organizational traditions. Be sure to include practices that are not in the policy or procedure manual, but which tend to guide operational practices. Compare your list of traditions to the principles discussed in this book: Are there any traditions that could restrict the implementation of TQM? What could you do to change or eliminate the restrictive traditions?

• Conduct an informal assessment of the distribution of authority and responsibility in your organization. Ask fifteen employees what they are responsible for in the day-to-day operation of the business; then ask the employees if they have been delegated enough authority to effectively accomplish each responsibility. What can you do about any discrepancies you discover?

• Observe the leaders in your organization. Do they merely talk about TQM, or do their actions demonstrate an understanding and commitment to its principles. Assess your own actions: Do you consistently make decisions that reflect an honest resolve to create an environment of continuously improving quality? What can you do to help the other leaders in your organization? What can you do about your own actions?

• How many communications systems (newsletters, meetings, bulletin boards, one-on-one contact, rumors, etc.) operate in your organization? Which system provides employees with the most accurate information? Which system provides the least accurate? What can you do to improve the least effective system? What can you do to maximize the most effective system?

CHAPTER 7

SIX TQM TECHNIQUES

Many of the techniques commonly used to implement TQM are standard training methods. In most organizations, the techniques are stand-alone elements of an overall management development program. In recent years, many of these techniques have been described in books, seminars, and convention talks, so information about them is available. They are not smoke and mirror techniques; they are time-tested methods of improving organizational effectiveness.

If there is a trick to these techniques, it is in applying several methods at the same time to one group. Persons experienced in management development have learned to stagger the techniques to prevent overwhelming or confusing participants. Also, it is not likely that implementation of TQM will require use of all six techniques, because each organization's needs are different. It is necessary, however, to determine which techniques will work best for a particular organization.

TECHNIQUE ONE: EMPOWERMENT

Without delegation of both authority and responsibility, empowerment fails.

To understand empowerment, it is first necessary to understand delegation. There is a substantial difference between a manager who routinely delegates tasks to subordinates and a manager who delegates to subordinates the authority to complete certain tasks. Unfortunately, some managers fail to delegate the authority to accomplish a delegated task. Effective delegation means to really let go. Delegating authority is perceived by some managers as giving up some-

56

thing, or losing control. But the manager doesn't "give up" anything; the responsibilities are shared, so others can perform also.

Therefore, empowerment is the transfer, or delegation, of both authority and responsibility. Without delegation of an equal proportion both authority and responsibility, empowerment fails. Employees who are given the responsibility for a task but not the authority to accomplish it will flounder. Likewise, employees who are given authority without responsibility can cause a disaster. The problem with managers "really letting go" has more to do with delegating authority than with delegating responsibility.

Empowerment has gained a bad reputation in some organizations, especially where it has been used inappropriately. Consider the manager of a retail store who tells a cashier he or she is responsible for handling cash register voids, merchandise returns, and customer refunds, but who fails to define how much authority the cashier has to handle those special transactions. The cashier must either call the manager to approve each special transaction or be able to read the manager's mind. In either event, the cashier becomes frustrated and does not perform to the manager's expectations.

In contrast, consider the manager who not only delegates responsibility for handling special transactions but also defines for the cashier precisely how much authority she or he has in handling them. The cashier then knows how to do the job—how far he or she can go in solving a problem. The cashier is less likely to become frustrated and more apt to meet the manager's expectations.

Empowerment works best if four forces are operating simultaneously:

1. The delegator (manager) has established a clear vision of where the organization is heading and what the goals are, and has communicated this to subordinates.
2. The delegator has established high personal and busi-

ness standards and has consistently demonstrated those standards through his or her actions. Employees learn more by watching their managers than they do by listening to them.

3. The delegator has established a strong working relationship with subordinates and trusts them to make wise decisions. This includes both expressing disappointment when performance expectations are not met and giving praise when they are achieved. A trusting boss-subordinate relationship can be established over time with good, frequent, and open communications.

4. The delegator is willing to let subordinates make mistakes, and only intervenes to prevent a disaster. Most people learn more from making minor mistakes, but workers are hesitant to make decisions if they fear retribution.

Effective empowerment defines not only an employee's responsibility but also the authority granted to act in specific matters. It's no secret that the communication of specific responsibilities is faulty in American business today. When properly applied, empowerment can be a powerful way to delegate specific responsibilities.

TECHNIQUE TWO: EMPLOYEE PARTICIPATION AND INVOLVEMENT

Tom Peters said that "the chief reason for [American industry's] failure in world-class competition is [its] failure to tap [the] work force's potential."[1] The all-to-frequent practice of excluding employees from the decision-making process is dangerous for two reasons. First, decision quality is decreased without the involvement of employees from different levels in the organization. The assumption that only manag-

1. Tom Peters, *Thriving on Chaos: Handbook for a Management Revolution* (New York: Knopf, 1988), p. 286.

ers know enough to make decisions reflects a mind-set that employees do not have the capacity to solve problems. This, in turn, sends the message that employee ideas are not valuable to the organization. When frequently reinforced, this mind-set defines strict boundaries between employees and management; it perpetuates a management versus employees adversarial relationship. It also can be a self-fulfilling prophecy, with employees beginning to believe they are not capable of making decisions or solving problems.

A person's position and job performance to a large extent determines what he or she is in other aspects of life. A person can tolerate being a mediocre bowler on the company bowling team, but that person cannot tolerate being a mediocre human being. Persistent exclusion from decisions and activities only reinforces the belief that workers aren't important. Feeling unimportant then leads to an "I don't care" attitude, which interferes with a company's providing the highest quality products and services.

There are three ways to expand employee participation and involvement in an organization. First, take a hard look at the regularly scheduled meetings and notice who attends them. In many organizations, meeting attendance is based on a person's position on the organizational chart. All managers attend one meeting, all department heads attend another, and all officers attend the weekly staff meeting. Rather than basing attendance on an arbitrary factor of position or title, consider including persons who could possibly contribute to fulfilling the purpose of the meeting. Or follow a rotating schedule of hourly workers who can attend as special guests. With a little sensitivity and understanding, hourly workers can become contributing members of these meetings.

Second, create a task force composed of both management and hourly employees to address a critical issue. Too many organizations exclude hourly workers from task forces because they are not "management." But that thinking merely perpetuates division in the company. Hourly employees selected to sit on a task force will feel honored to be included, and with encouragement will become involved in the group's activities.

Third, improve the ability of all employees to listen. Most people have the capacity to listen, but regrettably too few practice good listening skills. Management can listen better by providing the encouragement and the means for workers to speak up, to make suggestions and become involved, without fear of reprisal. Suggestion boxes and informal meetings with key executives can provide an excellent means to stimulate communication. Individuals can listen better by learning and using active listening skills. One of the most important skills a person has is how to listen well. It makes the person not only a more effective worker but also a more effective parent and spouse. Wise managers realize this need and help workers develop their listening skills.

TECHNIQUE THREE: CREATIVITY AND INNOVATION

Most managers don't understand, and often fear, the effects of creativity and innovation. In its simplest form, creativity is the destruction of established ways and methods. Most managers have been trained to hold on to established ways of doing things, so the idea of destroying those ways is foreign to them. Likewise, innovation can appear bizarre to managers from the "old school." After all, employees receive training to help them perform in established ways, not to experiment with new methods.

Art Cornwell, one of the best creative thinkers in American management today, said:

> Our education and experience to date has been based on the idea that there is a benefit in thinking like others have thought before us. As a result, we are taught the information generated by great thinkers in hopes of emulating them. One mental

skill which has not been developed is our ability to use illogical thought processes.[2]

Valuing or respecting contrary ideas is a principle that must be infused into an organization by its leaders and managers. It must be conveyed through the beliefs and actions of managers and supervisors as they not only encourage contrary ideas but also openly praise divergent thinking.

There are many barriers to the flow of creativity and innovation. Overcoming these barriers is the true test of an organization's ability to adapt TQM philosophy. Speaking on these barriers, Cornwell said,

> The most significant restraint to your creativity is your reliance on historical information. Your ability to think more creatively is dependent upon your skill in using this historical information to generate new ideas, rather than letting historical information limit your mental flexibility.[3]

TECHNIQUE FOUR: MANAGEMENT BY SCORE KEEPING

One of the greatest lessons in managing others can be found in a volleyball game at a company picnic. Before the game starts the group divides into two equal-size teams and checks the equipment. Players insist on reviewing the rules. Every player quickly learns the boundary lines, what constitutes a point, and how many points will win the game. Quickly, the game is organized and ready to play.

That's when the action begins! Players dive for the ball and hustle for shots; there is much laughter, and before long everyone works up a good sweat. Team members cheer good shots and offer advice and encouragement for ineffective attempts. Very soon team loyalty is obvious.

Valuing or respecting contrary ideas is a principle that must be infused into an organization by its leaders and managers.

2. Art Cornwell, *Freeing the Corporate Mind: How to Spur Innovation in Business* (Rockford, Ill.: The Boardroom, 1992), p. 77.

3. Ibid., p. 37.

Every player keeps score and is constantly aware which team is winning. Team members know if a player isn't pulling his or her load, of if he or she isn't playing by the rules. Players are highly motivated to win, and few stop playing hard until the outcome is decided.

Students of human behavior marvel at such displays of effort, commitment loyalty, and effectiveness, but few have applied the enthusiasm of a company volleyball game to the workplace. Author and speaker Charles A. Coonradt has said, "People will pay for the privilege of working harder than they will work when they are paid."[4] Said another way, employees are prone to work harder at recreation than they will work on the job. Coonradt noted that the secret of increased productivity on the job is to tap into the enthusiasm for recreation.

Every player in the volleyball game knows the score. A good shot that yields a point is immediately rewarded with an increased score. Indeed, the feedback is immediate for both positive and negative behaviors. Players are able to adjust their actions based on what happens to the ball and to other players. The secret, Coonradt says, is in the frequency of the feedback.

In too many American businesses, employees are denied frequent feedback. Some managers believe that providing no feedback is an indication of satisfactory performance. They seem to be saying, "If I don't tell ya otherwise, then you're doing OK." That is like hitting the volleyball over a brick wall with no way of knowing if it landed within bounds, or like shooting an arrow at a target while wearing a blindfold.

Coonradt added that "The appropriate amount of feedback can only be determined by the recipient, not the giver." That is contrary to many of today's management systems, which provide feedback once a year in a performance appraisal. Effective managers have learned the power of frequent and positive feedback. To tap into the motivation for

4. Charles A. Coonradt, *The Game of Work* (Salt Lake City: Shadow Mountain Press, 1984), p. 1. (800) 438-6074.

recreation, prepare two or three scorecards that graph specific results for each employee or group of employees. Determining what specific result to score and how to set up the scorecard can be challenges, but with a little experimentation they can be done.

Thomas S. Monson said, "When performance is measured, performance improves. When performance is measured and reported back, the rate of improvement accelerates." Monson's observation is important to understanding the power of feedback and scorecards. He says that when people know their performance is being measured, they improve their performance. Following that, when feedback is given performance accelerates even more.

TECHNIQUE FIVE: TEAM BUILDING

When several people work together to achieve a well-defined goal, the results of many far exceed the results of few.

For several years, trainers in team-building seminars have used a particular group activity. The participants are given a list of National Football League team names that have been disguised. For example, the name Seven Squared is the disguised name for the San Francisco '49ers. Another is Iron Workers, which refers to the Pittsburgh Steelers. Some of the disguised names are fairly easy to detect, such as King of Beasts, for the Detroit Lions. But several are difficult, such as Six Rulers for the Vikings. (It takes a few minutes to figure that one out.)

The participants are first asked to uncover the twenty-eight team names individually. Then they share their answers in small groups of three to five people. Finally, the facilitator brings the entire group together to share answers.

The exercise is a great demonstration of the importance of teamwork in making decisions. Individually, most people correctly name eleven team names; in small groups, the number increases to about twenty, and when a large group of at least twenty-five people share their answers, participants are able to uncover all twenty-eight team names. Participants learn that two heads really are better than one, and that when several people work together to achieve a well-defined goal, the results of many far exceed the results of few.

It takes skill to create teams in the workplace. It's not as simple as bringing several people together and calling them a team. And it's not permitting people to work together and believing they are a team. Team creation and management are challenging tasks that take practice to master. The group dynamics of assembling different personalities with different abilities and agendas can be overwhelming to an inexperienced team leader.

There are six work-related situations when using teams will improve performance, solve problems, or upgrade the quality of decision making:

1. When the problem is complex or not easily understood
2. When psychological ownership is desired
3. When there is a desire for improved decision quality
4. When improved team spirit and morale are needed
5. When there is a desire for improved communications
6. When there should be increased cohesion among team members

There are six situations when it is usually not advisable to use teams to solve problems:

1. When time is critical
2. When the solution is obvious or routine
3. When it is a one-person issue
4. When it is a disciplinary issue
5. When the problem involves an individual performance deficiency
6. When the solution is quantitative rather than qualitative

The team leader is an important element in building an effective team. The leader's ability to keep the team directed toward obtainable goals is paramount. There are six leadership behaviors that help promote more effective team performance:

1. Create an environment of open and honest communications
2. Help team members realize that agreeing to cooperate is important
3. Obtain commitment from each team member to work as a team
4. Reinforce that the task to be accomplished must dictate the procedure
5. Be diligent to forge workable compromises when differences appear
6. Be alert for opportunities to teach and direct

The members of an effective team commonly experience feelings of psychological ownership in the organization. That is, these team members think of themselves as stakeholders in the organization, and they gauge their behavior as if they were owners. The transition from just a member of a team to team member is both seen and heard. Team members with psychological ownership do the little things that help the organization be successful. They refer to the organization as "our" or "my" company and say "we" rather than "you," "your," and "their." They tend to work as hard as necessary to experience personal and organizational success.

In recent years there has been much talk about self-directed work teams (SDWTs). Some organizations, both public and private, have launched full-scale programs to convert their operations to SDWTs. These teams have been a frequent topic at conventions and association meetings, and have received much media interest as well. The problem is that autonomous or independent SDWTs can undermine a TQM philosophy. Management must ensure that team leaders understand both team and organizational goals; otherwise, the teams can become highly competitive and work contrary to a productive TQM culture.

Organizations that are driven to produce high-quality products and services have learned that all managers and leaders need periodic skills development.

TECHNIQUE SIX: MANAGER SKILLS DEVELOPMENT

Most people fail to see this obvious method, or understand how it relates to quality improvement. However, the stronger the management team's ability to manage and lead others, the better will be the quality output of the organization. Every organization, regardless of size or history, must have a comprehensive program to develop and improve its managers. If not helped to sharpen their managerial skills, most managers will develop ineffective or unproductive habits, and these habits can become a serious threat to a company's TQM philosophy.

There are many negative cultural and societal influences on management. For example, an autocratic style intimidates workers and creates an adversarial relationship between management and workers. It creates a climate of fear: fear of change, fear of experimentation, fear of speaking up, and fear of being wrong.

Organizations that are driven to produce high-quality products and services have learned that all managers and leaders need periodic skills development. Marriott, for example, has a five-year plan for its top managers that includes classes, seminars, and reading lists. Disney has similar plans for managers to ensure that managers develop effective interpersonal, discipline, leadership, and coaching skills.

WHAT YOU CAN DO

Following are statements about the six TQM techniques. Rate each statement as it applies to your organization:

5 = Completely True   2 = A Little True
4 = Mostly True   1 = Not True
3 = Somewhat True

Rating

1. Workers in our organization have been empowered to make necessary decisions that might affect the quality of products and services.   _____

2. Workers at all levels in our organization are given opportunities to participate in decision making.   _____

3. Workers at all levels in our organization are able to express their creativity without fear of criticism.   _____

4. Workers in our organization can track and display their job performance to be seen by themselves and others.   _____

5. Workers in our organization are able to share ideas and work together to solve problems in an open and honest environment.   _____

Total   _____

To score, add the points from the five statements:

20–25: TQM principles are working reasonably well.
15–19: TQM principles could be improved.
Less than 14: TQM principles need improvement.

HINTS TO HELP, IF YOU SCORED LESS THAN 20 POINTS:

• Observe the decision-making process in your organization to determine who has the authority to make critical business decisions. Has the authority been reserved at the highest levels, or have critical powers been delegated to the lowest and most convenient level? What can you do to empower workers to make critical decisions?

• As you observe the decision-making process in your organization, do you see certain levels of workers completely left out of the process? Are workers from all levels invited to participate in open discussions that will lead to a critical decision? What can you do to increase the involvement of workers from all levels into discussions and meetings?

• Pay close attention to the points of origin for the best ideas in your organization. What level do they come from: workers, supervisors, managers, or leaders? If they mostly originate with managers and leaders, you are missing the best ideas! Develop a plan to include workers and supervisors in a free-flow of ideas and suggestions. Work hard to eliminate criticism of any idea, regardless of how foolish it may sound.

• Ask fifteen employees in your organization if their job performance is better today than it was yesterday. Regardless of the answer ("yes," "no," or "I don't know"), ask how they know. Most people will respond with, "I don't know." When people don't know, performance remains stagnant and doesn't improve. Only when people know where they stand each day can performance improve. Help workers develop daily performance graphs that directly couple desired results with available resources.

• Develop a habit of listening as much to where suggestions come from as with the content of the suggestion. The direction of the suggestion is as important as the suggestion itself. Only when there is a constant upward movement of suggestions can an organization begin to know what must be done to achieve continuous improvement.

CHAPTER 8

TQM TOOLS

Quality is inseparable from the statistical tools used for its measurement and documentation. People trained in TQM tools do not use them just to solve quality problems. Rather, these tools enable them to build a quality incentive into every work activity. This means that quality is a basic element of the work processes; it is not a tool to solve a temporary problem. Likewise, TQM tools cannot be tacked on to a process through corrective or remedial actions. They must be an integral part of the program designed to achieve the highest possible quality.

TQM tools are used to control variability, which is the amount of difference from a predetermined standard or objective. *Business Week* reported that quality is "simply the absence of variation." Thus, the purpose of TQM tools is to eliminate or reduce controllable sources of variation in products and services. Uncontrolled variability is the heart of technical incompetence; controlling variability increases the possibility that the output will be improved. Ignoring variation, or tolerating its existence, is therefore contrary to the basic principles of TQM. Using TQM tools to control variability means that random change need not apply, since workers understand the work processes and can take action to control and improve them.

TQM tools are methods for collecting and then displaying data. Management information systems (MIS) reports often are columns of data that can appear meaningless to the untrained person, and sometimes even to the trained eye. Most people can better understand a chart or graph than a

There are thousands of hourly workers, in many countries, who understand and use standard TQM tools in their daily work.

traditional management report. That's why the basic tools of TQM, such as graphs, charts, and diagrams can be understood with little training.

Most of the TQM tools are based in statistical process control (SPC), which sounds more technical than it really is. Interpretation and application of these tools can become technical, but certainly need not be. There are thousands of hourly workers, in many countries, who understand and use standard TQM tools in their daily work.

SEVEN STANDARD TQM TOOLS

Since the beginning of the TQM movement, seven standard tools have been commonly discussed and used. They are the foundation upon which most other tools have developed.

Control Charts

Control charts display the results of statistical process control (SPC) (see Figure 3). They provide a visual means of knowing if a product or activity is within normal specifications. Few measurements on a control chart fall close to the mean or average tolerance. Most data points are either above or below the average or mean line. The average difference of random measurements (data points) from the overall mean is called the *standard deviation*. The standard deviation shows the extent of the variability.

Control charts include two additional lines for interpretation of data. They are the upper control limit (UCL), and the lower control limit (LCL).

> Ninety-nine percent [of the data points] will fall somewhere between +3 and −3 standard deviations from the mean. That is, one would almost never find a case of a measure so high, so far above the mean, as to be more than three times the average difference from the mean. Nor would one

Figure 3. In a control chart, a series of data points creates a line that is a visual representation of what happened to the individual elements in a process. Each data point is a single reference or measure of quality.

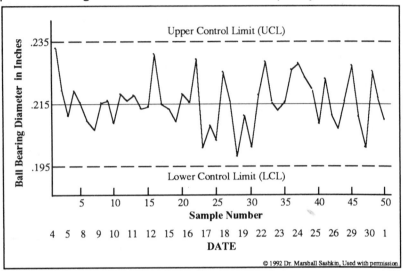

expect to obtain a measure so low as to be below the mean by more than three times the average difference from the mean. So +3 standard deviations is referred to as the Upper Control Limit (UCL), while −3 standard deviations is called the Lower Control Limit (LCL).[1]

Even when the distribution of data points on a control chart shows that the process is apparently in control, the average of the points could still be too high or too low. Even the amount of variation could be greater than desired. A control chart can help you identify what is causing those conditions so that they can be corrected.

Pareto Charts

Vilfredo Pareto was a nineteenth-century Italian economist who studied the distribution of wealth in society. He noted

1. Marshall Sashkin and Kenneth J. Kiser, *Putting Total Quality Management to Work* (San Francisco: Berrett-Koehler Publishers, 1992), p. 170.

that a small proportion of the population accounted for a large proportion of the wealth. This lead him, and others, to discover that in a surprising number of other situations, 80 percent of results are caused by 20 percent of causes. Eighty percent of a manager's time, for example, is usually spent dealing with 20 percent of his or her employees. Eighty percent of a company's profit often comes from 20 percent of its product line. Eighty percent of corporate loss usually stems from 20 percent of its products. Since then, this Pareto principle is recognized as a standard management principle around the world, and has been used in almost every aspect of business.

A Pareto chart displays the number of defects or problems over a specific time in a bar chart (see Figure 4). Managers use Pareto charts to attack the few 20 percent of causes that are responsible for the majority (80 percent) of their quality problems.

Figure 4. A Pareto chart illustrates that the majority of quality problems in a process are usually the result of a minority of causes.

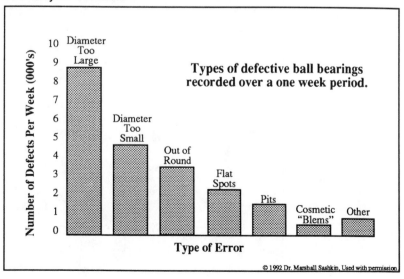

© 1992 Dr. Marshall Sashkin. Used with permission.

Fishbone Diagrams

Fishbone diagrams are also known as Ishikawa diagrams to some quality consultants because they were first developed by Kaoru Ishikawa. The problem or defect is shown at the head of the chart, with branches from the backbone indicating potential causes and effects in four major categories: machines, techniques, materials, and manpower (see Figure 5). A fishbone diagram can help illustrate how various problems affect each other. It has been widely used as a teaching aid in quality workshops, and it can help workers understand the relationships that must be controlled in order to improve quality. Managers have used fishbone diagrams to begin discussions of the causes of quality problems.

Run Charts

Run charts have also been called trend charts and line graphs. Magnitude or quantity is displayed on the vertical (y) axis, and time is represented on the horizontal (x) axis (see Figure 6). The magnitude scale should be expanded to a point

Figure 5. The fishbone diagram helps focus attention on the most likely causes of quality problems.

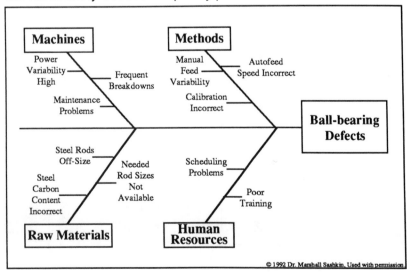

© 1992 Dr. Marshall Sashkin. Used with permission

Figure 6. A run chart is the accumulation of several data points from a control chart. A control chart shows the quality of each unit, and a run chart shows the quality of many units within a specific time frame, such as a shift or a day.

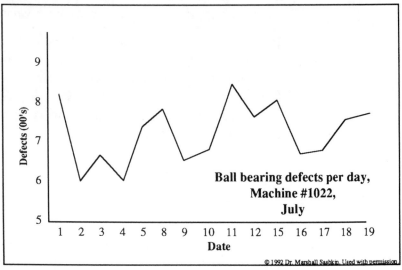

Ball bearing defects per day, Machine #1022, July

© 1992 Dr. Marshall Sashkin. Used with permission.

where changing data create a dramatic swing in the actual line. It is the nature of most people to want things to improve, which they can see as the line moves up. Time on the horizontal axis can represent hours, shifts, days, or even weeks.

A run chart is essentially a running tally of data points over a specific time reference. It is usually used to find critical times or periods when various problems are prone to occur. For example, much has been written about the quality of American vehicles manufactured in Detroit during the 1970s on Mondays and Fridays. A simple run chart would have graphically illustrated that problem, had anyone cared enough to collect the data and graph it.

Histogram

A bar chart is another name for a histogram. On a histogram, the number of products in each control category is displayed on a bar. By orienting the bars next to each other, comparisons can be easily shown (see Figure 7). The user can see which categories account for the most measured values, as well as the comparative size of each category. In many situations the bars will appear roughly in the shape of a bell; other times the pattern may be varied.

Because bar charts are one of the standard printing options on most electronic spread sheets, they have become fairly common in the business world. Experts on creating performance scorecards, such as Charles A. Coonradt, have discovered that bar charts are not as motivational to most people as line graphs.

Scatter Diagrams

Scatter diagrams get their name from the seemingly scattered appearance of the data points (see Figure 8). They are, however, an excellent quality tool that can illustrate how one aspect of a product relates to an apparently different aspect. For example, the scatter diagram could show how the hard-

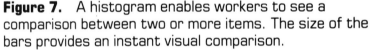

Figure 7.   A histogram enables workers to see a comparison between two or more items. The size of the bars provides an instant visual comparison.

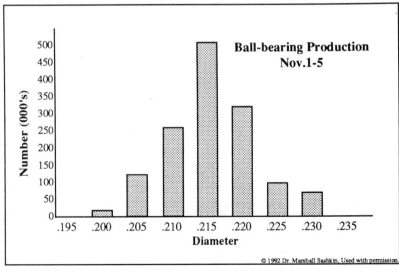

© 1992 Dr. Marshall Sashkin, Used with permission.

Figure 8. A scatter diagram illustrates the relationship between two values, such as how the quality of the raw material affects the quality of the finished product.

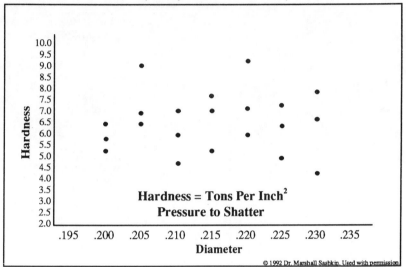

ness of a raw material relates to the roundness consistency of the manufactured product. As with many TQM tools, using scatter diagrams to their full value requires creativity and wisdom by the user. Beyond their design, owing to the scattered appearance of the graph, the other challenge is accurate interpretation of the information. Managers should experiment with scatter diagrams to develop the skills to fully use this valuable tool.

Flow Charts

Flow charts have also been called input–output charts because they are a visual representation of the steps in a specific work activity (see Figure 9). Many flow charts use similar symbols to refer to specific types of activities, which are illustrated in boxes. The type of symbol used isn't important, as long as the words convey accurate and universal understanding of that element in the process.

Managers using TQM principles have found flow charts very helpful in understanding how a process works and how it

Figure 9.   A flow chart graphically displays the sequence of events and options within a larger process. Flow charts can provide an excellent perspective on the overall process.

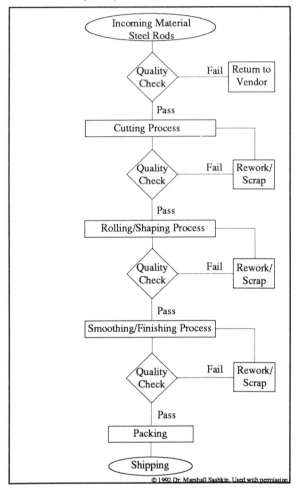

© 1992 Dr. Marshall Sashkin. Used with permission

can be improved. Flow charts can be an excellent training tool to describe how a new procedure could be applied to an existing process.

NEW TQM TOOLS

Discussions of new tools always seem to focus on their pros and cons. Perhaps this is because TQM tools do not consti-

Managers must be willing to experiment, modify, and adapt to find the most effective tool for their situations.

tute an exact science. A tool that works well in one situation may not work at all in another. Managers must be willing to experiment, modify, and adapt to find the most effective tool for their situations.

Many of the new tools developed since the original seven, discussed in the previous section, were created by the Japanese. They have led the way with TQM and TQM innovations. Genichi Taguchi developed the design of experiments (DOE) approach, which has been labeled the Taguchi method. Dorian Shainin, another Japanese TQM guru, disagrees with Taguchi and believes that his methods are superior. Still other experts believe that fault tree diagrams or affinity diagrams provide the best information. The constant evolution of TQM tools in Japanese organizations is an excellent example of the TQM principle of continuous improvement. It seems that no tool is without change; every one is a candidate for improvement or modification.

A new tool currently in use in a few American organizations is quality function deployment. It is a method of ensuring that the concern for quality is distributed throughout an organization as new products and services are designed, engineered, and introduced. Instead of adding concern for quality after a product has been designed and engineered, quality function deployment uses quality as a primary focus, beginning with conception and development.

Several of the new TQM tools involve sophisticated statistical analysis techniques, such as factor analysis. Many of these new statistical tools are a product of the expanding computer software market, which has introduced dozens of high-power programs to analyze and interpret data. Certainly, the number and quality of new statistical analysis tools will continue to increase in the coming years.

TQM tools not only help identify what is happening in a process but also point to possible causes.

PITFALLS IN USING TQM TOOLS

TQM tools not only help identify what is happening in a process but also point to possible causes. Managers who incorporate TQM tools into their operations soon learn that focusing on symptoms rather than causes is the greatest stumbling block to improving quality. Even experienced managers find it difficult to distinguish between symptoms and causes. Yet it is critical to identify the causes, or a manager can spend an entire career chasing elusive symptoms.

Organizations can be complex structures of individual personalities, with formal and informal lines of authority, policies, and procedures. Most people become protective of their territory, and as a result, sometimes view situations through an emotional curtain that clouds their objectivity. Numerous managers have had difficulty using TQM tools because of persons who may be affected by the data. It is vital, therefore, that any TQM tool be introduced in such a way that it will not be perceived as a threat, to either those persons who will use it or those who could change the results. One of the best ways of reducing emotional attachments to existing techniques or procedures is to explain why the tool is important, and then teach people how it can be used. Then let the workers discover for themselves what the data look like on the graph. This discovery process helps create psychological ownership of the tool and reduce potential opposition to its use.

Too often, TQM tools become the primary focus of TQM efforts. When this happens, there might be a few fragmented improvements in quality in a few isolated departments, but the overall TQM effort fails. This isn't to say that TQM tools are unimportant or can't be effective. Indeed, if used properly they are important and can be quite effective. But they must be only one element of an overall TQM strategy. All employees need not learn to use all the tools; rather, the tools are part of an entirely new system of management.

When a group of workers, a department, or an entire organization focuses primarily on tools, they ignore what else is necessary to create continuously improving quality. Too much emphasis on the tools can prevent people from understanding and dealing with the far more important principles of TQM, such as exceeding customer expectations and changing the organizational culture.

WHAT YOU CAN DO

Following are statements about TQM tools. Rate each statement as it applies to your organization:

5 = Completely True   2 = A Little True
4 = Mostly True   1 = Not True
3 = Somewhat True

Rating

1. Workers in our organization have access to the information that could be used to create TQM charts and graphs. _____

2. Information that could be used to create TQM charts and graphs is available to workers in a timely and prompt manner. _____

3. Workers in our organization use several traditional TQM tools. _____

4. Workers in our organization receive training in statistical process control. _____

5. Workers in our organization are encouraged to develop their own tools to improve quality. _____

Total _____

To score, add the points from the five statements:

20–25: TQM principles are working reasonably well.
15–19: TQM principles could be improved.
Less than 14: TQM principles need improvement.

HINTS TO HELP, IF YOU SCORED LESS THAN 20 POINTS:

• Conduct an informal assessment of the distribution patterns of information in your organization. Does most information tend to flow horizontally (within the managerial and/or executive level), or does it flow vertically through several levels? Ask several workers what information they "officially" and regularly receive, where it comes from, and if it is enough to perform their job adequately. Ask what they would like to receive. What can you do to improve the flow of information?

• Ask fifteen workers in your organization if they receive critical information on time. Ask them how much the communications process would have to be improved to increase their effectiveness. Compile the responses and make a report in a staff meeting.

• Make a list of the traditional, and nontraditional TQM tools, and then ask fifteen employees if they use any of them. Compile the results. You may want to use visual examples of the tools to facilitate easy identification. Compile the results into a list of tools and their application by person or department. Discuss the results of your survey in a staff meeting.

• Find out what has been done to train employees in statistical process control in your organization. Is there an ongoing program of orientation and training to ensure that employees can use the process to monitor and control quality? What can you do to help?

• As you survey the use of TQM tools in your organization, pay close attention to unique or specially designed tools. Make a list of creative uses of tools and share the list with other managers.

CHAPTER 9

MAKING TQM WORK

Making TQM work is not easy but it is possible, and it is certainly one of the most fascinating and rewarding challenges in management. TQM isn't a universal solution, so it can't be applied in the same manner in every organization. It isn't a one-time seminar or workshop that can be "installed" in an organization. It isn't something that can be learned by attending a single seminar, or by reading a magazine article or book. And it certainly isn't a tool that can be implemented overnight.

TQM can be confusing because it is really a dozen or more principles that make up a philosophy of management. So being able to make TQM work isn't as easy as teaching employees assertive communications techniques. Any TQM application demands customization of techniques and tools, based on a solid understanding of governing principles; there is no such thing as "one size fits all." In other words, making TQM work can be a challenge that demands patience and commitment.

There are many TQM "experts" expounding ideas and speaking in esoteric terms that few understand. These people don't educate the managers and business leaders who sense a profound need to improve quality in order to compete globally. But with so much talk about TQM, managers and leaders need to learn what they can do. The critical importance of TQM dictates that it be communicated in clear and understandable terms.

It is difficult to learn the principles of TQM by only studying theoretical ideas. TQM consists of two foundational elements: the theory and the practice, or hands-on experience in implementing that theory. This chapter isn't a complete guide to implementation. Rather, it is a compilation of implementation steps that have been used successfully by some organizations. Because every organization and every management team is different, every implementation must be customized. Realize that mistakes will be made, but a belief in the principles and persistence in the effort are keys to success.

Most failures at TQM implementation can be traced to a lack of either belief in the principles or commitment to the project by top-level management. A company's leaders cannot cancel the TQM effort just because the changes cannot be immediately cost-justified. Although TQM can produce results in a month, the quest for total quality improvement is a two-to-five-year project. And even when improved quality is realized, continuous improvement remains a never-ending process. This fact is contrary to many organizations and managers, who function on the basis of short-term decisions and short-term results. TQM demands long-range thinking and long-term planning.

TQM demands long-range thinking and long-term planning.

Successful implementation of TQM requires a *calculated*, *coordinated*, and *comprehensive* effort from the entire organization. It must be calculated in that it is intentional, not an outgrowth of some other management program. The intentions of the organization and its leaders must be *so* calculated that they are obvious to all managers, workers, vendors, and customers. The TQM effort must be coordinated among workers, supervisors, managers, and officers. The effort must move through the organization in a coordinated and systematic manner; there can be few, if any, isolated pockets of resistance to change. And the TQM effort must be comprehensive in that it includes not just one or two techniques or tools, but as many as possible, in as many areas of the organizations as is practical.

WHAT NONMANAGEMENT CAN DO

Any attempt by nonmanagement workers to implement TQM will have little or no impact on organizational culture. Management philosophies are a product of organizational culture, so nonmanagement workers have virtually no significant influence on culture or philosophy.

However, nonmanagement workers can have an impact on product and service quality. In truth, hourly workers have more potential to greatly influence day-to-day, short-term quality than does management, since workers are closer to the problems and their solutions. The problem is that most workers follow the example set by management, and achieve only the lowest level of management's expectations. If management doesn't drive quality and communicate specific expectations, most workers won't raise the level of their potential.

Nonmanagement personnel can be alert to honest attempts by the organization to improve quality or implement TQM. Because everyone has much to gain by improving quality, workers can reward management's efforts with constructive performance.

Nonmanagement workers can also exercise every opportunity to improve their job performance. Hourly workers should be encouraged to take advantage of elective training and educational opportunities. They should also be urged to increase the on- and off-job experiences that could have a positive impact on job performance.

There are many examples of hourly workers having asked probing questions of their managers which ultimately changed the course of the organization. If management elects not to ask questions of the workers or to involve them in the decision-making process, workers can ask questions of management. Obviously, some managers must be asked discreetly, but nonetheless the right question has the potential to change methods and be a catalyst for change.

WHAT MANAGERS AND SUPERVISORS CAN DO

Managers and supervisors can do more to improve quality than nonmangers, but they still only have a limited capacity to successfully implement TQM without complete support by the organization. Successful implementation requires a comprehensive and multifaceted approach. No single manager, or even a group of managers, can make it happen for an extended period of time in the entire organization. A sole manager can improve quality in his or her department, but even that might be temporary or restricted owing to interaction with other departments that have different agendas.

With the support and direction of upper management, however, managers and supervisors can do much to improve the quality of products and services in their departments. For example, they can learn more about TQM, dare to take risks, and try new techniques. They can be an example to their subordinates. They can resist the tendency to oppose change or hold on to the status quo. They can actively look for opportunities to experiment with new ideas, especially when suggested by subordinates. They can reward or recognize innovative thinking, especially when it comes from workers. They can be less critical of questions, comments, and suggestions, thus creating a climate for communication. Managers can believe that improved quality begins with individuals' changing their thinking and their actions. Managers must believe that change begins with themselves.

No goal is forever, and no specification is good enough to meet the demands or expectations of tomorrow's customers.

One of the most important TQM principles for managers and supervisors is the nature and critical importance of continuous improvement. Too often, managers believe that quality is a fixed goal set by specifications, and once it is achieved it need not be improved. Managers must believe that no specification or goal is fixed: Everything is subject to improvement. No goal is forever, and no specification is good enough to meet the demands or expectations of tomorrow's customers.

With or without upper management's support and direction, managers and supervisors can practice the six TQM techniques described in this text by implementing them in their departments. The techniques can be practiced individually, or more than one at a time. But any improvement in quality will require practice.

Managers and supervisors can teach quality to workers. They can explain why quality is critical to a successful operation. They can explain how the quality of products and services is directly related to job security. They can institute formal and informal training programs to improve job skills. And they can constantly search for ways to improve the overall abilities of their workers.

Managers can help workers develop a sense of pride, not only in the products and services they provide but also in the organization as an emotionally healthy place to work. Pride is best taught by example, so managers must be careful to never bad-mouth the organization; this includes its products, services, customers, and employees. Pride is taught by being a good communicator and explaining *why* things are done rather than *how* things ought to be done. *Why* is one of the missing ingredients in many managers' vocabulary. Charles A. Coonradt said, "To important people we tell 'why,' and to unimportant people we simply tell 'how.' People can tell how you feel about them by whether you tell them why or how."

One of the greatest hungers of the human soul is to be recognized as a valuable person, to be validated as a worthwhile employee. Regrettably, too many employees retire from well-meaning organizations without ever having been told how valuable they were to the organization. Too often, managers forget to express appreciation for consistency or superior performance. It is, perhaps, the single most effective way a manager can gain employee confidence and improve productivity and loyalty. It's important, therefore, for managers to devise systems to reward or recognize employees for their superior performance.

Managers must have a clear vision of what the goals are, and develop a front-of-mind awareness of how those goals can drive quality. They must develop a solid commitment to achieve goals and succeed. One such goal should be to develop systems and processes to create an environment that drives constantly improving quality. Another goal should be to design products and services that specifically meet customer needs and exceed their expectations. Too many managers believe that the primary goal is to successfully use TQM tools and techniques, and that has caused so many managers to become frustrated with TQM. Managers must believe that they can be successful in improving quality.

WHAT UPPER MANAGEMENT CAN DO

The most important initial element in quality improvement is the belief by the organization's leaders that success is directly connected to continuous quality improvement. Without that belief, all TQM efforts can meet only with marginal success. In contrast, the stereotypical American manager of the past believed that success was dependent on an autocratic management style—the philosophy "It's my way or the highway," meaning workers either do exactly as the manager wants or look for work elsewhere.

The leadership role for quality achievement must be assumed by more than one member of upper management. Two or more leaders espousing the same vision will have much greater impact. Obviously, the CEO is a key figure. He or she must openly and consistently support the quality movement, not only with words but also with actions.

After the leaders of the organization have developed consensus among themselves on the vision and purpose of quality, they must define policies and approve programs to put it in place. "The first responsibility of a leader is to define reality. The last is to say thank you. In between the two, the leader must become a servant and a debtor."[1] Every program must

1. Max De Pree, *Leadership Is An Art* (New York: Doubleday, 1989), p. 9.

specifically support the TQM philosophy; every policy must support the stated vision of quality; and every procedure must empower the workers to accomplish the task. Through policies, procedures, and programs, TQM principles will gradually become part of the day-to-day operation of the organization. But it is the leaders of the organization who must begin the process.

Buyers must be empowered to make decisions based on TQM principles.

Policies and procedures must be specific, in writing, and published in the organization. Policies must explain how the TQM philosophy applies to specific organizational practices, such as hiring, purchasing, or dealing with customers. For example, the purchasing policy should compare the value of accepting the lowest bid versus selecting a vendor based on the quality of raw materials or service. Buyers must be empowered to make decisions based on TQM principles, not on a predetermined procedure that demands selection of the lowest bid.

Upper management must be the true leaders of the quality movement. Anything but a sincere, honest commitment to quality will be apparent to workers and the movement will stall. This is one of the reasons why TQM is not a simple or an easy philosophy to incorporate. Many traditions must be broken so that quality-driven behaviors can surface.

W. Edwards Deming believed that the leadership role must include developing a customer-driven mentality. Unlike so many organizations that give only lip service to customer relations, being customer driven demands a total commitment to providing quality products and services, as defined by the customers, not the organization.

For example, in the early 1970s an electronics manufacturer grew from $1 million annual sales to $35 million in less than four years. The tremendous growth was a direct result of the company's listening to its customers and offering products that competitors didn't believe were possible or necessary. The CEO and founder of the company was the driving force behind this customer-driven movement—that is, until he decided that he knew better what his customers needed.

The company changed its direction from being customer-driven to being leader-driven, and its leaders, especially the CEO, stopped being sensitive to customer needs.

Several of the company's established products were changed; a few were dropped from the product line. A very expensive and radically new product was introduced, with an incredibly elaborate and costly advertising campaign. The press gave the new product a very poor rating. At a major trade show, engineers were unable to provide demonstrations for potential customers because the prototypes wouldn't work.

Being a customer-driven organization means just that: Customers make the key decisions that affect them most.

Sales of established products declined, sales of discontinued products ceased, and sales of the expensive new product were disappointing. In the face of disaster, the CEO maintained that the new product was the right direction to take, regardless of customer reaction and engineering's inability to make it work. As things went from bad to worse, he refused to change direction. Sales dropped from a record $35 million in 1974 to $8 million in 1975, a 77 percent decline in twelve months! Hundreds of employees lost their jobs, several key executives and engineers quit, the CEO was forced to resign, and the company was bought by a German organization. Being a customer-driven organization means just that: Customers make the key decisions that affect them most.

Being a leader typically means that subordinates will ask questions and seek approval for their actions. An effective leader must be an effective teacher. When asked a question or approval is sought for an action, a leader can answer the question with another question. "What do our customers want?" Or "What have you learned from our customers?" If the person asking the question doesn't know or is unsure of the answer, the leader can ask the person to come back when he or she knows the answer. This questioning process can be a great training exercise. It establishes the leader's role as gauging decisions based on customer needs.

Leaders must model TQM principles with their leadership behaviors. How leaders act is far more important than what they say, because subordinates emulate behavior more than they copy words. For example, the chairman of the board of one of the largest food and drug retail chains in America enjoys visiting his stores to get closer to employees and customers. He often complained, however, that his position and title got in the way of speaking to these employees and customers. As chairman, whenever he visited a store there would be a retinue of store, district, regional, and company executives following him around. He complained that the followers paid more attention to him than they did to the customers who were in the store. On one such visit, when the group was conspicuously large and was ignoring customers, the chairman excused himself and walked to a customer trying to get a particular patio chair from a large stack of chairs. He took off his coat and climbed over a smaller stack to select the color chair the woman wanted. After carrying the chair to the checkout, he returned to the group of embarrassed executives, put on his coat, and said, "Now, what do we get to see next?"

SUMMARY

This chapter has considered what can be done to improve quality by people at various levels of an organization. It is true that everyone in an organization can affect quality in one way or another. It is equally true, however, that managers and leaders can have a longer-lasting impact on policy than do hourly workers. The responsibility to see the vision and initiate the movement lies with an organization's leaders. The responsibility to sustain the movement on a day-to-day basis lies with the managers. And the responsibility for ensuring that quality improves lies with the hourly workers.

WHAT YOU CAN DO

Following are statements about how TQM can be implemented by various people in an organization. Rate each statement as it applies to your organization.

5 = Completely True   2 = A Little True
4 = Mostly True   1 = Not True
3 = Somewhat True

Rating

1. It is obvious to the workers in our organization that management's intention is to create a systematic and coordinated effort to improve quality. _____

2. Nonmanagement workers in our organization are provided opportunities to improve their competence and experience through well-designed training. _____

3. It is obvious to the workers in our organization that managers and supervisors understand what TQM is and how it improves quality. _____

4. Managers and supervisors take time to explain to workers why things work the way they do. _____

5. Policies and procedures in our organization are up-to-date, are published, and describe an effective process to drive constantly improving quality. _____

                                      Total _____

To score, add the points from the five statements:

20–25: TQM principles are working reasonably well.
15–19: TQM principles could be improved.
Less than 14: TQM principles need improvement.

HINTS TO HELP, IF YOU SCORED LESS THAN 20 POINTS:

• Observe the messages that flow from the executive and managerial levels of your organization. How many references are made to quality improvement? Are the messages sincere, or merely traditional quality hype? Are the messages consistent, unified, and coming from every level of the organization, or are they fragmented, inconsistent, and only from selected sources? What can you do to help the messages appear more consistent and comprehensive?

• Is job competence a high priority in your organization? An easy way to find out is to analyze the investment in budgeted dollars per employee for improved job skills for the past five years. Is the amount per employee consistent, is it increasing or decreasing, or does it vary significantly from year to year? What would it take to maintain a consistent program of improved job competence? Do you have the authority to make it happen?

• How accurate is TQM knowledge among management in your organization? If a TQM quiz was administered to the management team, what

(continues)

would the scores look like? If there were deficiencies, what would you do to improve the understanding of TQM? Why not try?

• Listen carefully to the conversations between supervisors or managers and workers. What percentage are "how messages" (managers telling workers *how* to do something), and what percentage are "why messages" (managers telling workers *why* things work the way they do)? If the how messages exceed the why messages—which is common in many organizations—what can you do to decrease the number of hows and increase the number of whys?

• Conduct an audit of your organization's policy manual. What percentage of the policies are current and up-to-date? How many policies involve quality? Do they reflect the principles of TQM, or are they merely admonitions about quality? Is your policy manual widely published in your organization? What can you do to improve the policies?

CHAPTER 10

TQM AWARDS, STANDARDS, AND CERTIFICATIONS

Numerous awards and certifications for quality have evolved in the past few decades. Although receiving an award for exemplary quality improvement or earning a certification for knowledge and understanding of quality certainly isn't necessary, many people enjoy these activities and are driven by them. This chapter briefly presents descriptions of a few better known awards and certifications for readers with that interest.

Note, however, that competing for quality awards merely to gain publicity or notoriety is not only a waste of the organization's resources but is also contrary to the basic philosophy of TQM. Quality products and services ought to be a natural outcome of decisions made in consensus, not by one or two individuals who seek personal fame or glory. In other words, change for the primary purpose of winning an award is change for the wrong reason. Changes ought to be made for the purpose of better serving customers, not for being recognized as a winner.

THE MALCOLM BALDRIGE AWARD

An act of Congress in 1987 established the Malcolm Baldrige National Quality Award. One or two awards are made each year in each of three categories: manufacturing, service, and small business. The purpose of the awards is to recognize U.S. companies that have demonstrated outstanding quality achievement and quality management. The Baldrige award is patterned after the Deming Prize, but the requirements and procedures are substantially different.

To apply for the Baldrige award, organizations must submit extensive documentation of their qualifications in seven major examination categories. Each category has two or more items, with a total of twenty-eight specific items. Categories and items are assigned a point value based on importance. The value of the items ranges from 15 to 75 points, and the seven categories of point values range from 60 to 300 points.

Applications are first reviewed by a panel of quality experts selected from business, professional, and trade organizations; accrediting bodies; universities; and government. A second review is then conducted by a second panel of three or more experts to determine which organizations deserve an on-site visit. The third review is conducted at the organization's facility and operating units by at least five members of the board.

Finally, the National Institute of Standards and Technology receives the findings and recommendations, and presents them to the U.S. Secretary of Commerce, who makes the final decisions.

The following chart shows the seven categories and the points allocated for each. There are two to eight items, with differing point values, for each of the seven categories.

1. Leadership	90
2. Information and Analysis	80
3. Strategic Quality Planning	60
4. Human Resource Development and Management	150
5. Management of Process Quality	140
6. Quality and Operational Results	180
7. Customer Focus and Satisfaction	300

The distribution of points among the seven categories is a commentary on the strategic importance of each category.

This book has stressed the importance of being customer driven, largely by determining and focusing on customer needs and expectations. That emphasis is obvious in the point total for the seventh category (Customer Focus and Satisfaction). Notice also that the fourth category (Human Resource Development and Management) has the third highest point total, and also has been stressed in this book.

Organizations that elect to pursue the Baldrige award must do so for the right reasons. Entering the competition can be time consuming and expensive. In fact, several organizations have suffered adverse effects in seeking quality awards. The Wallace Company in Houston, Texas, won a 1990 Baldrige award, but CEO John W. Wallace believes that the company's cost to share what it learned about TQM with other organizations contributed to the company's filing for Chapter 11 bankruptcy.[1]

THE SHINGO PRIZE

The Shingo Prize for Excellence in Manufacturing is designed to promote manufacturing excellence and recognize companies that excel in productivity and process improvement, quality enhancement, and customer satisfaction. There are two categories for prizes: large manufacturing companies, subsidiaries, or plants; and small manufacturing companies. The prize was established in 1988, and has achieved world-class status for its efforts in improving core manufacturing processes, implementing just-in-time philosophies and systems, eliminating waste, and achieving zero defects, while continuously improving products and decreasing costs.

The prize is awarded annually to companies in the United States, Canada, and Mexico that demonstrate manufacturing

1. Robert C. Hill and Sara M. Freedman, "Managing the Quality Process: Lessons from a Baldrige Award Winner," *Academy of Management Executive,* February 1992, pp. 76–88.

excellence, quality enhancement, and customer satisfaction. According to the application, "the Shingo Prize has become one of the most highly sought awards in American business, serving as a benchmark for companies who strive for the highest levels of quality, performance, and productivity."[2] The prize is designed so that the application process itself is a vehicle for improvement.

Applications are reviewed by a board of examiners, and high-scoring applicants receive on-site visits. On the basis of the review, the board recommends candidates to become prize recipients. The council reviews the recommendations and makes the final decision.

The following chart illustrates the evaluation categories and point distribution structure for the award.

1. Total Quality and Productivity Management Culture & Infrastructure (275 points)	
A. Leading	100
B. Empowering	100
C. Partnering	75
2. Manufacturing Strategy, Processes & Systems (425 points)	
A. Manufacturing vision and strategy	50
B. Manufacturing process integration	125
C. Quality and productivity methods integration	125
D. Manufacturing and business integration	125
3. Measured Quality & Productivity (200 points)	
A. Quality enhancement	100
B. Productivity improvement	100
4. Measured Customer Satisfaction (100 points)	100
Total Points	1,000

2. Arden C. Sims, president, Globe Metallurgical, Inc., quoted in "The Shingo Prize for Excellence in Manufacturing 1993–1994 Application Guidelines."

ISO 9000 REGISTRATION

In the early 1980s, the International Standards Organization (ISO) recognized the need for an international standard for quality management. In 1987, after considerable research and development, the ISO 9000 was developed and agreed upon by thirty-five participating countries. Since its introduction, over fifty countries have agreed to its standards. The ISO continues to add new elements to the agreement, so it is not a fixed set of guidelines.

ISO 9000 registration encompasses a series of standards that cover all aspects of an organization's operations. Most older organizations usually discover that they already comply with individual parts of the ISO standard, but they lack the documentation to verify their quality standards.

Most elements in the ISO 9000 are interrelated, so it's difficult to work on one element without dealing with related elements. Most quality experts and users of the ISO 9000 believe this is an advantage since the effort constitutes a complete or comprehensive quality system.

There are two basic purposes of ISO 9000 registration. First, it ensures that customers receive the product or service that they ordered; second, it guarantees that the process of supplying the product or service is carried out in the most efficient and cost-effective manner possible.

ASQC CERTIFICATION

The American Society for Quality Control (ASQC) was founded in 1946 and has over 125,000 members worldwide who promote, design, advance, or implement the cause of quality. Members have diverse professional backgrounds and functions, but are united in the cause of improving product and service quality. ASQC members are engaged in many facets of quality assurance, quality management, and quality engineering. The association's mission is to be "recognized as the worldwide leader in the advancement and promotion of quality concepts."

The ASQC offers a number of certification programs for its members. A certification is formal recognition by ASQC that an individual has demonstrated proficiency within and comprehension of a specified body of knowledge. Certifications are currently available in the following areas: quality engineer, quality auditor, quality engineer-in-training, quality technician, and mechanical inspector. The ASQC offers a variety of training courses to assist its members in gaining certification. Throughout the year, dozens of courses are offered on a wide variety of subjects.

APICS CERTIFICATION

The American Production Inventory Control Society (APICS) is an organization of more than 70,000 professionals primarily concerned with manufacturing and materials management. The association promotes total quality, global competition, and innovative manufacturing principles and practices through numerous education programs, publications, certification programs, and a not-for-profit foundation.

To further its cause of increasing industry education, APICS administers over 50,000 certification exams each year in three major certifications: certified in production and inventory management (CPIM), certified fellow in production and inventory management (CFPIM), certified in integrated resource management (CIRM). APICS can be an excellent source of not only technical information and solutions to problems but also for support through local chapters and participation in international conferences and exhibits.

GLOSSARY OF TERMS

ASQC (American Society for Quality Control) Offers a number of certification programs for its more than 125,000 members who demonstrate proficiency within and comprehension of a specified body of knowledge. ASQC offers a variety of training courses to assist its members in gaining certification.

APICS (American Production Inventory Control Society) An organization of more than 70,000 professionals primarily for manufacturing and materials management. The association promotes total quality, global competition, and innovative manufacturing principles and practices.

assessment (audit) A systematic and independent examination to determine whether quality activities and related results comply with planned arrangements and whether these arrangements are implemented effectively and are suitable to achieve objectives (ISO 8402). While used synonymously with the term audit, an assessment is often considered a collection of audits.

audit (external) (see *assessment*) An audit performed by persons outside the organization to ensure quality systems.

audit (internal) (see *assessment*) An audit performed by persons within the organization to ensure quality systems.

Baldrige award One or two awards that are made each year in each of three categories: manufacturing, service, and small business. The purpose of the awards is to recognize U.S. companies that have demonstrated outstanding quality achievement and quality management.

control chart Charts that display the results of statistical process control, which provide a visual method of knowing if the product or activity is within normal specifications.

culture A cumulative perception of how an organization operates and how employees treat each other, vendors, and customers. Organizational culture is constantly evolving and is largely a product of the values and perceptions of its leaders.

customer   Both internal and external buyers who are users of an organization's products or services.

Deming, W. Edwards   An industrial engineer considered to be the father of production quality and quality control. He developed what is known as the Deming cycle: Plan, Do, Check, and Act (PDCA).

employee participation   A technique to involve employees in the decision-making process. Participation is used to improve the quality of decisions by capitalizing on the knowledge and experience of many employees.

empowerment   The transfer, or delegation, of both authority and responsibility to others for the purpose of moving the source of power closer to that person who can use it most effectively.

fishbone diagram   A diagram that illustrates a problem or defect at the head of the chart, with branches from the spine indicating potential causes and effects in four major categories: machines, techniques, materials, and manpower. Also called an Ishikawa diagram.

flow chart   A visual representation of the various steps in a specific work activity. Flow charts can be helpful in understanding how a process works and how it can be improved.

histogram   A bar-chart display of the number of products in each control category. By orienting the bars next to each other, comparisons can be made to measure values and compare the size of each category.

ISO (International Standards Organization)   International organization headquartered in Geneva, Switzerland, and composed of the national standard organizations in over ninety countries.

ISO 9000   A series of international standards established by the ISO for the purpose of improving quality relationships between vendor, manufacturer, and customer. ISO 9000 includes standards that encompass all aspects of an organization's operations. Most elements within ISO 9000 are interrelated, so it is difficult to work on one element without dealing with other related elements.

Juran, Joseph M.   A contemporary of W. Edward Deming who had a significant influence on quality improvement. His greatest contribution has been described as defining and teaching methods of creating a customer-oriented organization. Juran taught that a focus on quality for the customer must be designed into every process and system in a company.

Pareto chart   Displays the number of defects or problems over a specific time in a bar chart. Managers using Pareto charts are able to attack the few (20 percent) causes that are responsible for the majority (80 percent) of quality problems.

quality   The totality of features and characteristics of a product or service that bear on its ability to satisfy stated or implied needs (ISO 8402).

quality assurance   All those planned and systematic actions necessary to provide adequate confidence that a product or service will satisfy given requirements for quality.

quality circles (QCs)   A group of employees brought together in a series of meetings (usually once a week) to discuss methods to improve the quality of products and services within an organization.

quality control   The operational techniques and activities used to fulfill requirements for quality.

quality council   A group of interested persons selected from all levels of the organization, brought together to identify potential barriers to adoption and implementation of a TQM philosophy.

quality management   That aspect of the overall management function that determines and implements the quality policy (ISO 8402).

quality manual   A document that identifies an organization's general quality policies, procedures, and practices.

quality policy   The overall intentions and direction of an organization concerning quality. The policy should be formally expressed by top management in a written document (ISO 8402).

quality system   The organizational structure, responsibilities, procedures, processes, and resources for implementing quality management (ISO 8402).

registration   Official indication that a supplier adheres to the ISO 9000X standards. The term is often interchangeable with the term "certification."

run chart   Trend charts and line graphs that display magnitude or quantity on the vertical (y) axis, and time on the horizontal (x) axis. Run charts show the actual occurrence of events as data points and lines.

scatter diagram   Diagrams that illustrate how one aspect of a product relates to an apparently different aspect. A scatter diagram could show how the hardness of a raw material relates to the roundness consistency of the manufactured product.

service   The results generated by activities at the interface between a supplier and its customer, and by the supplier's internal activities to meet the needs of subsidiaries, plants, or small manufacturing companies.

service delivery   Service delivery is the supplier's activities necessary to provide a service.

Shingo Prize   Award designed to promote manufacturing excellence and recognize companies that excel in productivity and process improvement, quality enhancement, and customer satisfaction.

team building   A technique of improving morale by increasing team spirit. In TQM, team building can be an effective means of creating employee involvement and commitment to principles.

Total Quality Management (TQM)   An organization's management philosophy to attain customer satisfaction through a comprehensive program of tools, techniques, and training.

TQM tools   The devices used in TQM to identify and correct problems with quality. They commonly include graphs, charts, and diagrams.

TQM techniques   Methods used to integrate TQM tools into an organization. Traditional techniques include team building and empowerment skills.

INDEX

American Production and Inventory Control Society (APICS), 100
American Society of Quality Control (ASQC), 99, 100
assessments, 14, 22, 37, 46, 55, 82, 94
authority, 45, 49, 68
awards (TQM), 95

Baldrige National Quality Award, 16
banners, 16
bar chart, 73
behavior, 25

certification, 95
change resistance, 43, 55
continuous improvement, 14, 86
control chart, 26, 27, 28, 62, 71, 72
Coonradt, Charles A., 3, 33, 76, 87
Cornwell, Art, 60, 61
creativity, 60
CSAI, 37
culture (organizational), 18, 23, 24, 46, 52
customer service, 16, 17, 34
customer surveys, 37

delegation, 45, 56, 57
Deming, W. Edwards, 7, 12, 29, 31, 43, 89
Deming Prize, 96
Deming's fourteen points, 8, 9, 10, 11
Deming's seven deadly diseases, 11, 12
design-of-experiments (DOE), 79
Disney, Walt, 24, 66

employee involvement, 58, 68
employee participation, 58, 59

empowerment, 2, 45, 49, 56, 57, 68, 89
excellence, 2

fear, 9
feedback, 28, 33, 62
fishbone diagram, 74
flow chart, 77, 78
focus groups, 38

goals, 3, 17, 86

histogram, 75, 76
human resource development, 96

innovation, 60
integration, 51
International Standards Organization (ISO), 99
ISO 9000, 99
Ishikawa diagrams, 74
Ishikawa, Kaoru, 74

Juran, Joseph M., 12

Kiser, Kenneth J., 5, 46, 72

line graph, 72
listening, 60, 69, 94
lower control limit (LCL), 27, 71, 72

Marriott Corporation, 66
mass inspection, 8
mission statement, 25, 32
Monson, Thomas S., 63

National Football League, 63
National Institute of Standards and Technology, 96
Nordstrom's, 24, 39

Pareto chart, 72, 73
participatory management, 29
PDCA (Deming Cycle), 7, 29
Peters, Tom, 35, 58
power, 49
production quality, 7

quality circles (QCs), 6, 7, 17
quality control programs, 19, 21
quality council, 49, 50
quotas, 10

run chart, 74, 75

Sashkin, Marshall, 5, 37, 46, 47, 72
scatter diagram, 76, 77
score keeping (management), 61
self-directed work teams, 65
Shainin, Dorian, 79
Shewhart, Walter, 29
Shingo Prize for Excellence in Manu-
    facturing, 97, 98
standard deviation, 71
statistical process control (SPC), 29,
    71, 82

strategic quality planning, 96
suggestion box, 36

Taguchi, Genichi, 79
Taguchi method, 79
team building, 2, 63
team leader, 64, 65
TQM techniques, 5, 28, 33, 51, 56
TQM tools, 5, 26, 33, 51, 70, 78, 79,
    80
TQM training, 5, 9, 30
TQMAI, 46, 47
Tunks, Roger, 9

upper control limit (UCL), 27, 71, 72
Urquhart, John, 52
U.S. Secretary of Commerce, 96

values, 23, 24, 32
variability, 26, 34, 70

Wallace, John W., 97
Wal-Mart, 24
Walton, Sam, 24
Williams, Richard L., 37